Becoming Fully Human in an Inhuman World

Becoming Fully Human in an Inhuman World
The Why, What, and How of Spiritual Formation

Knofel Staton
with
Cathryn Comeaux

Wipf & Stock Publishers
Eugene, Oregon

BECOMING FULLY HUMAN IN AN INHUMAN WORLD
The Why, What, and How of Spirtual Formation

Copyright © 2005 Knofel Staton. All rights reserved. Except for brief quotations in critical publications or reviews, no part of this book may be reproduced in any manner without prior written permission from the publisher. Write: Permissions, Wipf & Stock, 199 W. 8th Ave., Eugene, OR 97401.

Unless otherwise noted, all Scripture quotations are taken from THE HOLY BIBLE: THE NEW INTERNATIONAL VERSION

ISBN: 1-59752-498-0

Manufactured in the U.S.A.

DEDICATION

In Appreciation

To

John and Dorothy Cachiaras

And

In Memory

Of

Glen and Ethel Staton

Contents

Introduction ix

Chapter 1. The God Who is For Us 1

Chapter 2. The Human Connection with The Divine Creator 12

Chapter 3. The "Godufactured" Shattered 22

Chapter 4. God's Preparation for the Restoration of Humanity 33

Chapter 5. The Global Need: God with Skin On 44

Chapter 6. Jesus: The Restoring God 55

Chapter 7. God's Goal for Us 64

Chapter 8. Needed: Spirit-Filled Leaders 72

Chapter 9. Transforming into Christlikeness: Part One 84

Chapter 10. Transforming into Christlikeness: Part Two 97

Chapter 11. How Then Shall We Live?	111
Chapter 12. How Then Shall We Feel	122
Chapter 13. Before We Get to Heaven, We Can Become Like Him	132
Chapter 14. How Then Shall We Commit?	141
Chapter 15. There Never Was Another: Christ is Worth Representing	147
Appendix 1. Issues to Ponder and Apply from Each Chapter	153
Appendix 2. An Eleven-Week Program Engaging Spiritual Disciplines	166
Appendix 3. Assessing Personal Spiritual Formation Into Christlikeness	205

Introduction

To grow old in Christ without growing up into Christlikeness is a systemic malfunction in the Church, which has reached epidemic proportions. Spiritual formation is not just important, but is also essential for individual Christians if the Church will effectively impact its local and global world for Christ.

Movies, television, books, and videos have shaped our concept about what it means to be human. Probably many of us have said something like this about a person who really messed up morally, "After all, that person is only human." But from God's vantage point, that is not accurate. That's being inhuman. Peter described people who lived relationally and morally dysfunctional lives as being like "unreasoning animals" (2 Peter 2:12, NASB). To function like animals is not to live according to our created kind. We should say something like this, "The reason a certain person is so kind, loving, forgiving, compassionate, generous, peaceful, joyful, gentle, unselfish, patient, faithful, trustworthy, and under control is because that person is fully human and living like it in an inhuman world."

We live in a culture that relationally is saturated with moral relativity, and religiously is surrounded with polytheism. In such a culture, it is not difficult to give our culture more influence to shape our life more than the church. Consequently, the media outside us may have more influence than the Master inside us, unless we are maturing spiritually. Humans were "Godufactured" according to God's kind, so we could and would relate according to God's ways. To do so is to be fully human in an inhuman world. This book develops what it means to be fully human; why should we be, and how can we be?

The book goes beyond most books on spiritual formation by beginning with the nature of the Triune God, who has always existed in community, moves to the nature of humanity created in His image and likeness, and how individuals can mature to functionally relate as God does. Three appendixes include relevant pondering questions with practical applications for each chapter, an eleven-week practical program for spiritual formation, and a comprehensive assessment tool for measuring progress.

Chapter one reveals the relational nature of God within the community of the Trinity as the model for community living on earth, which is possible by God creating humans in His own image and likeness. Chapter two develops the relational nature of humans who were given God's character equipment for proper relationship through the breath of Life, God's own relational Spirit. Because God's grace is greater than the disgrace after sin permeated this planet, God called His people to privilege—what He wants to do to us, and to purpose—what He wants to do through us, which is to be a blessing to all categories of people on earth. Blessing all kinds of people through God's people is God's continual conspiracy against Satan (chapter three).

Because God's people neglected the purpose side of His call, God prepared for our restoration (chapter four). Because humans did not live like God, God decided to live like a human on earth in Jesus, who modeled what God is like on one hand, and how to be fully human in an inhuman world on the other hand (chapter 5). In Christ, fallen humanity can be restored to God's original creation in order to become fully human in an inhuman world (chapter 6).

God's goal for people re-connected to Him through Christ is that we continuously change in order to be conformed to the likeness of Christ by the equipment of the indwelling Spirit, by being helped by Spirit-filled leaders and Spirit-filled friends in a Spirit-filled community—the Church (chapters 7 and 8). Chapters nine and ten introduce eleven different spiritual disciplines that are powerful for transforming us into becoming fully human. Chapter eleven discloses several lifestyle dimensions of people in whom Christ intimately lives, while chapter twelve shares

Introduction

several spiritual and physical benefits of being connected to Christ. Chapter thirteen affirms that people can mature into Christlikeness before getting to heaven, while chapter fourteen calls for our commitment to be who we are as human created according to God's kind, and chapter fifteen paints a broad picture of the awesomeness of Christ from whom becoming fully human radiates.

This book is biblical, relational, understandable, and applicable. It is targeted for individuals, who want to mature into being fully human, for small groups the members of which can help each other, and for entire congregations to study and apply.

Civilization becomes fully humane only when humans act and react according to our created kind in Genesis, which is recreated in Christ.

Scattered throughout this book are practical ways to measure how close we are to becoming conformed to the likeness of God—thus becoming fully human in an inhuman world.

May this book be a tool for bringing more of heaven to earth through those "Godufactured" according to God's kind in order to relate according to His ways.

May this book honor the Father, Son, and Holy Spirit, and may you, the reader, put a smile on God's face by applying it in your life for your maturation into Christlikeness.

> Knofel Staton and Cathryn Comeaux, co-thinkers and co-producers of *Becoming Fully Human in an Inhuman World*.

1

The God Who Is For Us

Have you ever wondered just what kind of God we have? We have an inside glimpse of certain aspects of His nature with the first four words in the Bible, "In the beginning, God . . ."(Genesis 1:1). Those four words report essential aspects about God. "In the beginning" reveals that God existed before anything else. Not only does the beginning relate to the nature of God, but also **God Himself is the beginning.** He not only caused the "Alpha," He is the "Alpha," the first letter in the Greek alphabet, which became a metaphor for "beginning."

The God Who Always Was and Always Will Be

God is the Alpha who got it all started. Likewise, He is the Omega, the last letter in the Greek alphabet, that became a metaphor for the end of something. God will end all earthly existence as revealed in Revelation, "It is done. I am the Alpha and the Omega, the Beginning and the End" (Revelation 21:6; see also Revelation 22:13 and 1:8).

God Himself never ends. He is the eternal/everlasting God (Genesis 21:33). Everything about Him is everlasting—His mercy, grace, compassion, kindness, power, and so on. Anyone in whom God lives by His Spirit is also everlasting, because His Spirit is eternal (Hebrews 9:14; Galatians 6:8; Ephesians 2:22). God is eternal, as the Psalmist declared, "Before the mountains were born or you brought forth the earth and the world, from everlasting to everlasting you are God" (Psalm 90:2). God was never not God and will never not be God.

Earthly time is not headed toward nothingness, but toward God's goal. Our existence will not end when God destroys the solar system, but will continue its eternality either with or without God. Eternality cannot be calculated with earth-bound seconds, minutes, days, weeks, months, and years; thus one day in God's timeless environment will be like a thousand years in our time-bound environment, and a thousand years will be like one day. It will be as stated in the song Amazing Grace, "When we've been there ten thousand years, Bright shining as the sun, We've no less days to sing God's praise than when we'd first begun."

God is never not God and never will be

God Exists in and for Community

There are several different names for God in the Bible; however, none is His nomenclature that identifies Him from others as our names do. Instead each name is packed with various aspects of God's nature and function.

The first word for God in the Bible is the Hebrew word *Elohim*, which is the most common word for God throughout the Old Testament. *Elohim* is a plural word, and is used 217 times in the Old Testament. It not only refers to our One God, but also to the plurality of pagan gods. For instance, see Genesis 31:30; Exodus 12:12; 20:3.

Earthly time is not headed toward nothingness, but toward God's goal

Why is the same plural word for pagan gods also used for the Creator God, who was not, is not, and will never be plural, but was, is, and will always be one (Deuteronomy 6:4; Romans 3:30)? It is because God exists within a plurality of Himself—the Father, the Son, and the Holy Spirit.

From everlasting to everlasting God exists within a community—His triune Community. God has never been a "lone ranger", but has always been, is now, and will always exist within relationships. He is not the *deus solitarius* (solitary God), but is the *deus triurus* (triune God). He is "God-in-community." He is "God-for-community." He is the relational God—our community-related-God.

Life among those within the Trinity is **the** model for positive community relationships. Among the persons of the Trinity is unity amid diversity; mutuality of liberty, and love; individuality and interdependence; correspondence and cooperation; co-existence and community. Our awareness of the "communityness" of God is not gleaned from just the first biblical word for God or from the reality of the Trinity, but also from the fact that God expanded the population of heaven when He created innumerable angels, who witnessed the creation of the world (Job 38:7).

From God's relationships within community and His commitment **for** community, God created this world with community kinds of characteristics. Life on earth was created to be a micro-community that could mirror the heavenly community—unity with diversity, correspondence with cooperation; individuality with interaction; and co-existence with cooperation.

Life among those within the Trinity is the model for positive community relationships

The interdependent balanced design of this universe sprang from God's ecologically relational nature that characterizes the persons within the Trinity. The diverse aspects of this world were created to work with one another and for one another. Doing so is the way each individual element in nature is to co-exist with other elements. One micro example of that is the interdependent need of animals and plant life for each other. For instance, animals exhale carbon dioxide that is essential for plant life. After plant life interacts with the sun and water, it "exhales" oxygen that is essential for animal life. God designed each form of life to need some kind of interdependence with at least one other form of life. Because God was committed to a holistic earthly community, He designed each living form to be interdependent with and not independent from all other life on earth.

The entire cosmos was designed by God to exist as a community of diversity. Nowhere is that better seen than in the workings of the micro-community of the human body with the cooperative interdependence of each part relating with other parts for the health of the whole body. When that does not happen, "dis-ease" results, because something in the system is not in balance with something else in the system.

Our intelligent God did not have to create this universe the way He did. But because he lives in community and is for community, He designed this universe with its billions of intrinsic mammoth and microscopic essential interdependent functions, most of which we have probably not yet completely discovered or correctly understood.

God is Love

"God is love" (1 John 4:16). Agape-love is not just one of God's attributes, but love is His basic nature from which all His relational characteristics flow. It is a mistake to think that He **was** the God of law in the Old Testament, but **is** the God of love in the New Testament. God's basic love nature has never changed and saturates both the Old and New Testaments. Below are just few places of hundreds (130 times in Psalms alone) that speak of God's love in the Old Testament:

1. "He will love you and bless you and multiply you" (Deuteronomy 7:13, NASB).
2. "Yet on your fathers did the Lord set His affection to love them . . ."(Deuteronomy 10:15, NASB).
3. "He . . .shows His love for the alien . . ." (Deuteronomy 10:18, NASB).
4. "Since you are precious in my sight, since you are honored and I love you" (Isaiah 43:4, NASB).

The word *agape*-love appears many more times in the Greek translation of the Old Testament (*The Septuagint*) than it does in the New Testament. God was never not the God of love. His creation of this universe and His law are expressions of His love. Seven times the Old Testament is described as God's covenant of love (Deuteronomy 7:9,12; I Kings 8:23; 2 Chronicles 6:14; Nehemiah 1:5, 9:32; Daniel 9:4).

Love is God's basic nature from which all His relational characteristics flow

Because love is God's root nature, He enjoys loving as revealed in Micah 7:18, "Who is a God like Thee, who pardons iniquity and passes over the rebellious act of the remnant of His possession? He does not retain His anger forever, **because He delights in unchanging love**" (emphasis mine, NASB). The person with agape-love is never selfish, but always shares self with and for others. Our God, who is love, not only created a community of things, but also a community of people with whom He uniquely shared a significant part of Himself.

God is never not the God of love

God Shares His Nature

It was out of love that God created not only the nature around us, but also the nature inside us. God created humans with the capacity to not only accept and appreciate His kind of love, but also to apply His kind of love as the extension of God's love. **To love exactly as God loves is one way to measure how close we are to being conformed to the likeness of God, and thus becoming fully human in an inhuman world.**

God did not create life because He was lonely. There is no aloneness among the Father, Son, and Holy Spirit. Nor did God create angels and humans because He needed their help to take care of this planet, and to deal with whatever problems might develop. In Himself, (the interdependence of the Father, Son, and Holy Spirit) God is more than able to meet all needs in heaven and on earth, because He is God Almighty.

Humans are to function as the extension of God's love

As the Almighty God, He has unlimited power and freedom. On the one hand, He has power and freedom to be totally independent from anything or from any other being. On the other hand, out of His love He chose to create people to work alongside Him. So in that respect God decided to limit part of Himself to function in and through people. That self-imposed limitation is God's love sharing Himself with others. He does not need us for any reason except for the reason that love never exists in isolation. His nature is to love without the inherent need to be loved by anyone or anything beyond the persons within the Trinity who have unbroken mutual love with and for each other. By sharing His nature with others, we voluntarily join God's interdependent relationship for community.

Every time God created life in the first chapter of Genesis He used the same phrase ten times in less than two minutes of reading time. Why would anyone repeat himself that many times in such a short time? Perhaps that person is old, and from our solar timetable, God is certainly old; but that's not the reason for repeating that phrase. Perhaps that person is forgetful, and God is also forgetful, for He remembers no more the sins He forgives (Isaiah 43:25; Jeremiah 31:34; Hebrews 8:12; 10:17); but that's not the reason either. God can forget anything He intentionally remembers to forget. Doing that is evidence that His love is linked to His power, the power of self-control and grace.

God's "age" and "forgetfulness" had nothing to do with the repeated use of that phrase. Instead, it was God's way of using a hi-lighter, of underlining, of circling, and of shouting loudly, "I want you to get this before you read any further!" Here comes that repeated phrase:

1. God created plants **according to their various kinds** (verse 11).
2. God created vegetation **according to their kinds** (verse 12a).
3. God created trees **according to their kinds** (verse 12b).
4. God created sea life **according to their kinds** (verse 21a).
5. God created every winged bird **according to its kind** (verse 21b).
6. God created living creatures **each according to their kinds** (verse 24a).
7. God created livestock **each according to its kind** (verse 24b).

Three times in one verse (25) God used that phrase as if He was constructing a crescendo in His creational opus that was approaching the apex of His creative concert. Get ready for the blasts of trumpets, the standing ovation, the excited shouts from angels, and the display of heavenly fireworks as the outstanding activity of God's creation is about to reach its climax.

8. God created the wild animals **each according to its kind** (verse 25a).
9. God created the livestock **according to their kinds** (verse 25b).
10. God created all creatures **according to their kinds** (verse 25c).

Now bring on the heavenly brass band, the marching angels, and the sky full of fireworks, because for the first time when God created a form of life, He did **not** say, "according to their kinds" or "its kind." Instead, God said, "Let us make man in our image, in our likeness" (Genesis 1:26). God replaced "according to their kinds" with "in our image, in our likeness." That was God's way of saying, "Now I am not going to create man according to man's kind, but **according to my kind**." Notice the "us" and "our", which signal the mutual community relationship among the Father, Son, and Holy Spirit in creative activities (See the Spirit's involvement in Genesis 1:2, and the Son's in Colossians 1:15-16; John 1:2).

To be created in the image and likeness of the Trinity is to be relationally like God—people living in community and committed to community through God's kind of sharing love. To be in God's image is to exist as God's reflection throughout His cosmos. As we allow His kind of love to flow through us, He can see Himself in us, and so can others. Paul understood that when he wrote, "Be imitators of God, therefore, as dearly loved children, and live a life of love. . ." (Ephesians 5:1). We are to function relationally as God would and does, as Jesus reminded us, "Be merciful, just as your Father is merciful" (Luke 6:36), and as John wrote, "We love because He first loved us" (1 John 4:19).

To be in God's image is to live as God's reflection throughout His cosmos

Being in the likeness of God does not extend beyond our relational nature. We are not exact replicas of all there is of God. We are **unlike God** in more ways than we are like Him. Here are a few ways we are not like God:

1. We are not little gods (although at times we may try to act like we are).
2. We are not from everlasting.
3. We had a beginning.
4. We were not uncreated.
5. We were created.
6. We do not have unlimited freedom.
7. We do not have unlimited power.
8. We have physical bodies.
9. We will physically die.
10. We have limited knowledge and understanding.
11. We cannot give orders to nature that has to obey us.
12. We can be separated from the Father, Son, and Holy Spirit.
13. We are not part of the Trinity.
14. We get sick.
15. Whatever we are is given to us from God.
16. We are designed by God.
17. We cannot do miracles by ourselves.

While we are unlike God in most ways, accepting or not accepting the reality that humans were created in the image and likeness of God has significant ramifications for how we live on earth in at least two essential ways, both of which are relational: (1) how we value all people, and (2) how we treat all people. Every cultural development, such as political, philosophical, scientific, and so on; and every cultural benefit and service, such as health-related, education, work, and so on are rooted in our view of humanity's beginning.

People do not become fully human through civilization, but through God's original design of us in creation, and through His recreation of us in Christ. Civilization becomes fully humane when humans act and react according to our created and recreated kind, or it becomes inhumane if we do not.

The "man" that was created in God's image does not refer to just the male gender. The word "man" is from the Hebrew word *dama*, which is used three different ways in the Old Testament: (1) the male gender; (2) a person's nomenclature, such as the name "Adam" with "Eve"; (3) mankind or humankind. The New Revised Standard Version (NRSV) is more accurate by translating *dama* in Genesis 1:26 as "humankind" (See also TNIV).

Civilization becomes fully humane when humans act and react according to our created and recreated kind

Dama in verse 26 is a singular word (humankind), but is connected to a plural pronoun, "and let **them** rule over . . ." Why the plural pronoun **them?** Because the man/humankind created in God's image included both genders—male and female as seen in verse 27, "So God created humankind, in his image in the image of God he created them; male and female he created them" (NRSV). Genesis 5:1-2 clearly communicates this, " . . .In the day God created **man**, He made him in the likeness of God. He created **them** male and female, and He blessed **them** (male and female) and named **them** (male and female) **man** in the day **they** were created" (NRSV, bold print and "male and female" in parentheses are mine). Both genders share the same likeness of God, and thus the same value and dignity.

Six times during God's creative activity He looked at what He created and saw that it was "good." The Hebrew word for "good" is *tob*, which in Hebrew literature was used to describe several different situations: (1) something that is pleasant, such as a pleasant aroma; (2) something that makes sense, such as a neat idea; (3) something that is moral, such as a decent action; (4) something that is functioning according to its design, such as an effective car. When God saw that vegetation, plants, and fruit trees were good, he was not describing morality as if to suggest apple trees were not having some kind of kinky affair with corn stalks. God was not suggesting that sea life was not having immoral affairs with bird life. Six times God used "good" to describe that what He created was acting and reacting in accordance with its created design (Genesis 1:4,10,12,18,21,25).

The only time God declared something was not good in creation was when He saw the single male. Then God said, "It is not good for the man to be alone. . ." (Genesis 2:18). "Not good" in that verse describes the fact that without another human, Adam could not function according to his created kind, i.e., to live in and for community with an equal. No human can be fully human while living in isolation from all other humans. We need each other.

The God-for-Us

The first act of God for us was the creation of this universe. God created this universe for humans. He had us in mind when He developed the blueprint for His creation. Not the planet, but people were the determining factor behind the genius of God's architectural work, which He revealed in several places such as in Psalm 115:16, "The highest heavens belong to the lord, but the earth he has given to man." The entirety of Psalm 8 prioritizes people in God's creative work. Everything God created is for us and is beyond our understanding as Isaiah wrote, "Since ancient times no one has heard, no ear has perceived, no eye has seen any God besides you, who acts on behalf of those who wait for him" (Isaiah 64:4). Everything God created is for our enjoyment (1 Timothy 6:17). But we are not to enjoy it at the neglect of others.

Since God is filled with love, He shares that basic nature with us, so we can enjoy the pleasures He enjoys by loving as He loves through the "A" to "Z" (and many more) expressions of love with the following examples:

    A. To adore others and not abuse them.
    B. To bless others and not blast them.
    C. To cherish others and not compete against them.
    D. To delight in others and not demean them.
    E. To energize others and not eliminate them.
    F. To fulfill others and not forsake them.
    G. To grace others and not grieve them.
    H. To help others and not hinder them.
    I. To involve others and not impair them.
    J. To join with others and not jeopardize them.
    K. To be kind to others and not be a killjoy with them.
    L. To love others and not loathe them.

M. To maximize others and not minimize them.
N. To be nice to others and not nasty to them.
O. To optimize others and not oppress them.
P. To perfect others and not pervert them.
Q. To quicken others and not quench them.
R. To be reconcilers with others and not be revengeful toward them.
S. To serve others and not skip them.
T. To teach others and not threaten them.
U. To under gird others and not undermine them.
V. To value others and not be violent with them.
W. To work with others and not wrong them.
X. To be xenia (hospitable) for others and not "x-clude" them.
Y. To yoke with others and not yip with them.
Z. To be zany with others and not zap them.

To love exactly as God loves is one way to measure how close we are to being conformed to the likeness of God, and thus becoming fully human in an inhuman world

In summary, people were created to imitate God by living in community with His kind of love. Humans were "Godufactured" according to God's kind, so we could and would relate according to His ways.

While we do not know precisely how God created other forms of life "according to their kinds," we know how He created humans "according to His kind." And to that we turn in the next chapter.

Humans were "Godufactured" according to God's kind, so we could and would relate according to God's ways

2

The Human Connection With The Divine Creator

The Holy Spirit in Us

We do not know precisely how God created other forms of life, but in Genesis 2:7 we have a significant handle on how He created humankind, "the Lord God formed the man from the dust of the ground . . . ." Some stop reading right there, and seem to think it is normal to live like dirt. However, the fact that God used dust from the ground was His "show and tell" that we have an assigned relationship to this planet and an awesome responsibility for it. God designed our environment in such a way that if we take care of it, it will take care of us. Abuse it, and it will abuse us. Pollute it, and it will gradually poison us. Has God's people taken seriously the spiritual role of being caregiver managers of this planet?

Genesis 2:7 does not end with our connection to the cosmos, but with our connection to the Creator, " . . .and breathed into his nostrils the breath of life, and the man became a living being." That verse painted the picture of a non-living person who all of a sudden has someone else's life breathed into him. Whose life did God breathe into that man? God's own. But precisely what is "the breath of life" that entered Adam?

The word "breath" is from the Hebrew word *neshamah,* which is one of the two Hebrew words for "spirit." Job used the same word when he spoke about God's Spirit, "The Spirit of God has made me; the breath of the Almighty gives me life" (Job 33:4, NASB). The same word also described God's Spirit in Job 34:14-15, "If it were his intention and he withdrew his spirit and breath, all mankind would perish together and man would return to the dust." In these verses the words "spirit" and "breath" are parallel, i.e., interchangeable. God breathed into humanity His own Life—the Holy Spirit.

The Essential Nature of the Spirit

The Hebrew and Greek words for "Spirit" are also the same words translated as "breath." Why would God use the same word for His Holy Spirit that was commonly used for the "breath"? As breath is an indication that life exists, God's Spirit is the evidence of the presence of His life. God infused into Adam's mortal body God's own life. Only people who have God's Spirit will live forever, for " . . . if the Spirit of Him who raised Jesus from the dead dwells in you, He who raised Christ Jesus from the dead will also give life to your mortal bodies through His Spirit, who indwells you" (Romans 8:11, NASB).

The Holy Spirit is the presence of God's life

God used the same word for His Holy Spirit that was also commonly used for "wind", because winds are powerful. Winds can be the contributing force with benefits, such as water available from windmills, electricity from wind generators, and the power to move sailboats. But winds also can cause destruction, such as in a tornado or gusts up to 100 mph. As winds are powerful, so is God's Spirit, which is described biblically as "the power of the Holy Spirit", and " . . . a demonstration of the Spirit's power" (Romans 15:13; see also 1 Corinthians 2:4, and 1Thessalonians 1:5).

The Spirit as God's Presence

What aspect of God's life and power do we get when we receive the Holy Spirit? We certainly do not receive all the aspects of God's life and power. His Spirit in us does not make us another god. His Spirit does not enable us to create something out of nothing, nor call another universe into existence by our words. So what do we get with God's Spirit? We receive God's intimate presence. God's Spirit is paralleled (interchangeable) with God's presence as seen in the following texts (bold print is mine to more easily see the paralleled interchange):

1. "Do not cast me from **your presence**, or take **your Holy Spirit** from me" (Psalm 51:11).
2. "Where can I go from **Thy Spirit**? Or where can I flee from **Thy presence?**" (Psalm 139:7).
3. "I will ask the Father, and he will give you another Counselor to be with you forever—**the Spirit** of truth . . . I will come to you . . . **My Father** will love him, **we** will come to him and make our home with him" (John 14:16-24).
4. "Ananias, how is it that Satan has so filled your heart that you have lied **to the Holy Spirit** . . . ? . . . .you have lied . . . .**to God**" (Acts 5:3-5).
5. "And in him you too are being built together to become **a** dwelling in which **God** lives by his **Spirit**" (Ephesians 2:22).
6. "Therefore, he who rejects this instruction does not reject man but **God,** who gives you his **Holy Spirit**" (1 Thessalonians 4:8).
7. "And this is how we know that **he** lives in us: We know it by the **Spirit** he gave us" (1 John 3:24).
8. No one has ever seen **God**; but if we love one another, **God** lives in us and his love is made complete in us. We know that **we** live in **him** and **he** in us, because he has given us of his **Spirit**" (1 John 4:12-13).

Relational Characteristic of the Spirit

With the Holy Spirit, we have God's character equipment for proper relationships. Through His Spirit God transfers His own relational characteristics to us. As God is the relational God within and for community, so He created humankind to be relational with the characteristics of His Spirit. To relate as God does is one way to measure how close we are to being conformed to the likeness of God, this becoming fully human in an inhuman world.

With the Holy Spirit, we have God's character equipment for proper relationships

We see some of the relational characteristics of God's Spirit in Galatians 5:22-23, "But the fruit of the Spirit . . ." Fruit refers to the product or the yield of its source. There is an essential grammatical truth here, because "the fruit" is singular, but nine things are listed. The plurality of nine is connected to and flows out of the first attribute listed—love. Elsewhere Paul wrote ". . .God has poured out his love into our hearts by the Holy Spirit, whom he has given us" (Romans 5:5). The eight other listings in Galatians 5:22-23 radiate from love. The connection of love to the other characteristics is like a hub, which is love, and the eight characteristics are spokes extending from the hub. Each one is relational and enhances community, as seen in the following:

Love is relational. This kind of love (agape) always unselfishly gives for the benefit of others.

Joy is relational. Joy is weakened and diluted without love. John got at that when he wrote that early Christian leaders proclaimed Jesus to others "so that you also may have fellowship with us. And our fellowship is with the Father and with his Son, Jesus Christ. We write this to make our joy complete" (1 John 1:3-4). Joy reaches its completeness in community—in relationships—in fellowship with others and with the triune God.

Peace is not only the absence of warfare, but also the absence of animosity.

Patience describes someone who remains under difficult situations.
Kindness describes someone who is polite and respectful.
Goodness describes someone who would not do anything immoral to another.
Faithfulness describes a loyal person who would not violate another's trust.
Gentleness describes someone who is mild (not wild) when not getting what is desired or expected.
Self-control describes someone who is levelheaded and keeps his temper in check.

These are the relational characteristics of God who has always existed in community and is for community. God's plan is for His people "to keep the unity of the Spirit through the bond of peace"—His kind of community (Ephesians 4:3); and to imitate the Father by living a life of love—the relational foundation for initiating and maintaining community (Ephesians 5:1).

The Relationality of Christianity

Christianity is **the** relational religion. It is possible to either intentionally or unintentionally make Christianity too much head, and not enough heart; too much ritual, and not enough relational; too much legalism, and not enough "lovalism" (my coined word); too much being correct, and not enough being compassionate.

Christianity is the relational religion

Where do we get the idea that Christianity is **primarily** relational? We get it from God who shared His relational equipment with humans—the Spirit of Life. We get it from Jesus who violated many cultural and religious traditions of His day in order to demonstrate the relational nature of God and God's intention for His people. We also get it from the Law itself. There are 613 commandments in the Old Testament. One day some chaps teamed up to get Jesus into trouble by asking Him a test question, "Teacher, which is the greatest commandment in the Law?" Jesus did not hesitate to outline the relational nature of the Law, "Love (relational) the Lord your God with all your heart and with all your soul and with all your mind. This is the first and greatest commandment.". But Jesus did not stop there, "And the second is like it: Love (relational) your neighbor as yourself." ["relational" inserts are mine] Then Jesus dropped the bomb on the theology of Judaism when he added, "All the Law and the Prophets hang on these two commandments" (Matthew 22:36-40). What an explosive blast! Jesus was declaring that there is no commandment among the 613 that does not deal with proper relationships—with God, with self, with others, with things, and with the devil—not one. In Matthew 25:31-46, Jesus clearly communicated that when the world comes to its end, we all will be judged by proper and improper relationships demonstrated by what we did or did not do to help needy people with such essentials as food, drink, friendship, clothes, health-care, and attention. Cain's question, "Am I my brother's keeper?" gets a loud "yes" from Jesus' life and teachings (Genes 4:9).

When the world comes to it end, we will be judged by our proper and improper relationships demonstrated by what we did or did not do to help needy people

From Legalism to "Lovalism"

The reality that Christianity is relational is also gleaned from the legalist of all legalists in Jesus' day—Saul/Paul, who was "extremely zealous for the traditions" of Judaism (Galatians 1:14), and described himself as "a Hebrew of Hebrews; in regard to the law, a Pharisee; . . .as for legalistic righteousness, faultless" (Philippians 3:5-6). But in Christ Saul was converted from legalism into "lovalism". This is clearly seen by the fact that Paul did not write about law in every one of his letters, but he did about love as seen in the following examples:

1. " . . .he who loves his fellowman has fulfilled the law . . .. Love does no harm to its neighbor. Therefore love is the fulfillment of the law" (Romans 13:8-10).

2. If I speak in the tongues of men and of angels, but have not love. . . If I have the gift of prophecy and can fathom all mysteries, but have not love . . . If I give all I possess to the poor and surrender my body to flames, but have not love, I gain nothing (1 Corinthians 13:1-3).
3. "Therefore show these men the proof of your love and the reason for our pride in you, so that the churches can see it" (2 Corinthians 8:24).
4. "The only thing that counts is faith expressing itself through love" (Galatians 5:6).
5. "Be imitators of God, therefore, as dearly loved children and live a life of love . . ."(Ephesians 5:1-2).
6. "Then . . .. make my joy complete by being like-minded, having the same love, being one in spirit and purpose" (Philippians 2:2).
7. "My purpose is that they may be encouraged in heart and united in love . (Colossians 2:2).
8. "May the Lord make your love increase and overflow for each other, and for everyone else . . ."(1 Thessalonians 3:12).
9. "We ought always to thank God for you, brothers, and rightly so, because your faith is growing more and more, and the love every one of you has for each other is increasing" (2 Thessalonians 1:3).
10. "The goal of this command is love, which comes from a pure heart and a good conscience and a sincere faith" (1 Timothy 1:5).
11. "For God did not give us a spirit of timidity, but a spirit of power, of love and of self-discipline" (2 Timothy 1:7).

In addition to Paul's writings, love appears in every other book in the New Testament, as seen in the following examples:

1. "Love the Lord your God with all your heart and with all your soul and with all your mind. This is the first and greatest commandment. And the second is like it, 'Love your neighbor as yourself.' All the Law and the Prophets hand on these two commandments" (Matthew 22:37-40).
2. "Love the Lord our God . . . Love your neighbor as yourself. There is no commandment greater than these" (Mark 12:29-31).
3. "But love your enemies, do good to them . . ." (Luke 6:35).

4. "A new command I give you: Love one another. As I have loved you, so you must love one another. By this all men will know that you are my disciples, if you love one another" (John 13:34-45).
5. While the word "love" does not appear in Acts, it is practiced throughout Acts. For instance see 2:44-45; 3:1-10; 4:36; 5:12-16, and so on.
6. " Keep on loving each other as brothers" (Hebrews 13:1).
7. "If you keep the royal law found in Scriptures, 'Love your neighbor as yourself,' you are doing right" (James 2:8).
8. "Show proper respect to everyone: Love the brotherhood of believers, fear God, honor the King" (1 Peter 2:17).
9. ". . . make every effort to add to your faith . . .brotherly kindness, love" (2 Peter 1:5-7).
10. "No one has ever seen God; but if we love one another, God lives in us and his love is made complete in us" (1 John 4:12).
11. ". . his command is that you walk in love." (2 John 1:6).
12. "The elder, To my dear friend Gaius, whom I love in the truth" (3 John 1:1).
13. "Mercy, peace and love be yours in abundance" (Jude 1:2).
14. "I know your deeds, your love and faith, your service and perseverance, and that you are now doing more than you did at first" (Revelation 2:19).

The "Communityness" of Christianity

In every New Testament letter the writers shared ways to demonstrate love in specific situations. God wants His people on earth to live together in community as we would were we in heaven. By doing so, we would fulfill part of the prayer Jesus taught, "your will be done on earth as it is in heaven . . ."(Matthew 6:10). **To be fully human in an inhuman world is to act and react the way God would if He were here. And He is here by His Spirit in His people** (Ephesians 2:22).

I suspect most of us have said something like this, "The reason a person is so mean, so dishonest, and is not trustworthy is because he or she is only human." But being like that is not functioning according to our created kind, and so is not being as His "human." Without God's

Spirit, a person is a deficient, damaged, and an incomplete human who relates in inhumane ways. Movies, words of many songs, television shows, books, magazines, the Internet, video games, and much more have so saturated our culture with inhumane actions and reactions that many people believe those ways illustrate what being fully human is about. However, we should think something like this: "The reason that person is so nice, so patient, so forgiving, so kind, so honest, and so helpful, is because he or she is totally and wholly human and is living like it." To be fully human is to function in accordance with our relational nature—created in the image and likeness of God.

Why will a dog bark and a cat meow? Because each is acting according to its kind. Would my dog slip over to the neighbor's yard and steal a piece of meat left for their sleeping dog? Of course, because it is acting according to its kind. But when my dog got that meat back to our yard, would he repent and return it while thinking, "I can't do that to my dog-friend next door"? Of course not, because he is acting according to his kind. But would a person steal something from a neighbor and not take it back? If so, that person is not acting according to his/her created kind. And we should not think, "after all, he/she is only human." That is not being human, but is being inhuman. Why would a coyote "kidnap" a little rabbit for lunch? Because it is acting according to its own kind. But before biting into it, would that coyote look into those little eyes, and think, "I can't do that. I know the agony of a parent when one of the kids does not get home on time. So I'm going to escort you to your home, so no other animal will get you"? Of course not, because it is acting and reacting according to its kind. But would a person slip into a neighbor's house, kidnap a little girl, rape her, and kill her? Many have; however, do not even think," He's only human." That is not being human; it is being inhuman; it is being a deficient human. When Peter wrote that some people lived dysfunctional relational lives, he described them as living "like brute beasts" (2 Peter 2:12)—not living according to their created kind in the image and likeness of God.

We humans were created according to God's kind so we could and would relate according to God's ways. God created male and female to co-exist with loving expressions of mutuality and cooperative equality. Neither one was more or less in the likeness of God than the other one. God created both genders to be His representatives on earth. To be in

God's image is to reflect His character in relationships that include His kind of rule—the rule of love, not of an arbitrary master over another person. Being in the *imago dei* (image of God) is to relate to one another with care, compassion, and service. The *imago dei* person is an *analogia relationis*—an analogy of relatedness—God's relatedness.

God created the male and female to co-exist with loving expressions of mutuality and cooperative equality

Only after God created both male and female in His image and likeness, and they began to interact with each other, with God, and with creation did God change the "good" descriptions to "very good" (Genesis 1:31).

To relate as God does is one way to measure how close we are to being conformed to the likeness of God

Eventually something happened that shattered God's creation. And the "very good" turned into the "very bad."

To that we turn next.

3

The "Godufactured" Shattered

Privilege and Purpose in the Garden

Any coin from the U.S. mint has two sides to it (heads and tails) in order to be an authentic spendable coin. As with the coin, so it was with the two sides of God's creation of Adam and Eve. One side was **privilege**—what God did for them: the other side was **purpose**—what God wanted to do through them. The **privilege** side included the following:

1. Receiving God's own Spirit—His character equipment for proper relationships.
2. Being created in the image and likeness of God.
3. Freely participating with all the advantages of the Garden of Eden—the beauty of gold, onyx, the aromatic resin; companionship with the domestic animals; protection from the wild animals; and partaking of every tree in the garden, except one.
4. Enjoying the immediate presence of God with two-way companionship and communication.
5. Being given to each other.

6. Being informed ahead of time what would be harmful.
7. Having no competition from nature that would hinder their activities.

Their **purpose** side included the following:

1. Ruling over the fish, birds, and creatures that move on the ground. The word for "rule" is the same one used to describe God's caring and compassionate concern.
2. Cleaving to each other.
3. Having children in order to expand God's kind of community.
4. Working in the garden.
5. Taking care of the garden.

Community in the Garden

Adam and Eve enjoyed a perfect community of unity in the following relationships:

1. With God. They could walk and talk with God—authentic partnership.
2. With self. They were naked and not ashamed—good self-esteem.
3. With the other gender. Waking up and seeing Eve, Adam bragged about her, "This is now bone of my bones and flesh of my flesh . . ."(Genesis 2:23). He did not view her as a competitor, but as a companion; and not as his possession, but as his partner. He must have viewed her beauty instantly, for what a change she was from the animals, many of which were not all that attractive, and none as gorgeous as the woman.
4. With the natural environment. There were neither thorns nor thistles; evidently neither rains nor snows, neither air pollution nor poisoned water, neither earthquakes nor erosions, neither brush fires nor floods.

Freedom in the Garden

God commanded, "You are free to eat from any tree in the garden; but you must not eat from the tree of the knowledge of good and evil, for when you eat of it you will surely die." Why did God allow Adam and Eve to be tempted in the garden? The answer is captured in one word—"love." Authentic love does not force another's response, but liberates the one loved to decide whether or not to respond with love; to respond to caring with compassion; to respond to grace with gratitude; and to respond to companionship with complementation, not with competition. God wanted Adam and Eve to live with Him in the garden with friendship, fellowship, and "followship" not because they had to, but because they wanted to. Anyone who forces another to love does not love, but lords it over the other one. The result is not God's kind of community. God wants us to love because we are loved. He wants us to love gracefully and not grudgingly.

Authentic love never forces another's response, but liberates the one loved to decide

God created people with the capacity to freely decide between right and wrong; between good and evil; between love and hate; and between obedience and disobedience. Jewish rabbis are correct to teach that God created Adam and Eve with two different impulses or tendencies: a good impulse, *ha-yetzer-ha-tob,* and an evil impulse, *ha-yetzer-ha-ra.* Without the two impulses and the freedom to choose one over the other at any given time, we would not be the kind of person God created. Any good or bad we do would not radiate from our own decisions. Without both impulses and the freedom to choose, there would be no morality or virtue expressed from our voluntary intentional desires. We would not have the ability to choose love, patience, forgiveness, humility, and so on.

God created people with the capacity to freely decide between right and wrong

However, there could not be rational choices for right (*tob*) and wrong (*ra*) unless there were options and guidelines for making those choices.

Certainly the first three chapters of Genesis do not record the amount of time and the various ways God related to Adam and Eve, and the ways they related to each other, nor all of God's communication with Adam and Eve and their communication with each other.

Instructions in the Garden

Because God is Father as well as Creator, it is not unreasonable to suppose that He verbally taught and modeled how Adam and Eve should relate to Him, each other, animals, plant life, and the immediate environment. Surely He would have explained how to cultivate and care for the land. Likewise, He might have shared such relational insights as how to express their love to each other; how to verbally and non-verbally communicate admiration to the other person; how to share with each other without claiming that what is mine is mine, and not yours; and how to properly care for each other, notice each other, pay attention to each other, support each other, affirm each other, build up each other, honor each other, and respect each other spiritually, mentally, verbally, physically, and sexually.

Surely God did not create them and then just let them try to figure out on their own what being human is all about. After all, if small children need teaching and modeling about their relational actions and reactions, surely Adam and Eve, who had no other family except the Father, would need His input. I suspect between Genesis 1:26 and Genesis 3:1-7 the Father spent decades communicating and modeling to help Adam and Eve develop their relationships. Adam and Eve knew what was relationally good (*tob*) and what was relationally bad (*ra*). So being tempted to choose the bad versus the good involved more than a decision about the tree of the knowledge of good and evil. Being tempted also dealt with their primary choices about how to relate to God and each other, as do temptations we encounter.

Was their decision to eat or not eat from the tree of the knowledge of good and evil relevant for us today? Of course it is, because the reality of their choices relates to all people in all places for all periods. That tree represents any non-God source to which we may turn to get our concept of what is good and evil; what is right and wrong; what is moral and immoral.

The tree of the knowledge of good and evil represents any non-God source for determining what is right and wrong

We are to understand the difference between righteousness and unrighteousness from God and not from the "trees" of our peers, movies, music, videos, books, television, Internet, and our conscience unless those are linked to God's ways. To the degree that we depend upon other sources, we will substitute gadgets for God, cultural living for Christ-like living, alternative lifestyles for awesome lifestyles; concessions for commands; relativity for absolutes; and hellish conduct for heavenly conduct.

Two Kinds of Life and Death in the Garden

While the New International Version reads, "when you eat of it," the better translation is "in the day that you eat" (NASB, RSV, NRSV). God communicated that the result of eating from the tree would be sudden and sad, "You will surely die." But what kind of death would that be?

The primary nuance of "death" is separation. We communicate separation when we describe death with such terms as "departed, gone home, no longer here, passed on, and passed away."

There are two different kinds of death. I like to communicate the first kind of death with a small "d"—death. This is the physical or biological death that happens when the human spirit or breath leaves a person's body. I like to communicate the second kind of death with a capital "D"—Death. This is the spiritual Death that happens when God's Spirit or Breath leaves a person's body.

The capital "D" Death separates us from God's indwelling Spirit, and the result is that we are not fully human as we were created to be. Instead, we are deficient, incomplete, and damaged individuals. Our initial sin brings that kind of separation as reported in Isaiah 59:2, "But your iniquities have separated you from your God."

Anyone who dies physically (small "d" death) without God's presence inside will eternally exist where God is totally absent (capital "D" death). Hell is hellish because God is not there in any dimension as revealed in 2 Thessalonians 1:9, " They will be punished with everlasting destruction and shut out from the presence of the Lord and from the majesty of his power."

The "Godufactured" Shattered

The capital "D" Death separates us from God's indwelling Spirit, and the result is that we are not fully human as we were created to be

As there are two kinds of death, so there are two kinds of life. I like to describe the first kind with a small "l"—life. This is the person who is alive physically or biologically, but without God's Spirit. I like to describe the second kind of life with a capital "L." This is the person who is aLive physically, but also with God's Holy Spirit living inside—thus Living spiritually as well as physically.

We can easily see both kinds of life and death in many biblical texts, such as in the following two texts (My bold and capital letters correspond with the kind of death and life being described below):

> As for you, you were Dead in your transgressions and sins, in which you used to live when you followed the ways of this world . . .All of us also lived among them at one time, gratifying the cravings of our sinful nature. . . .. But because of his great love for us, God, who is rich in mercy made us aLive with Christ even when we were Dead in transgressions. . . .(Ephesians 2:1-5).
> For the wages of sin is Death, but the gift of God is eternal Life in Christ Jesus our Lord (Romans 6:23).

Everyone on earth lives in one of the following situations:

The small L inside the big D describes those who are physically alive, but spiritually Dead without God's Spirit. The small d with the big L describes those who have God's Spirit inside, but eventually will die physically. Given enough time the mortality rate for all of us is 100%. It is one small "d" physical death for all of us unless Christ returns first.

Sin in the Garden

It may have taken decades, but eventually Adam and Eve caved in to the allurements of the forbidden tree and the deceptions of the devil, who disguised himself as a snake (see Revelation 12:9 for the identification of the serpent as the devil or Satan). While many come down hard on Eve, I suspect most of us would be as attentive as she was if a snake began to communicate with us in understandable human words. Both Adam and Eve shared responsibility for their own disobedience as seen in 1 Timothy 2:14 that spotlighted Eve's sin, and in Romans 5:15-19 that spotlighted Adam's. Their sin and the resultant separation from God's indwelling Spirit turned their lives and the cosmos upside down The community of unity in the garden turned into the chaos of disunity, which was reflected through the following four human relationships:

1. **With God**, which changed from fellowship to fear. They hid from God, because they were afraid (Genesis 3:8-10). That was the beginning of all phobias on earth. Adam blamed God first, "the woman you put here with me . . ." (Genesis 3:12). That was the beginning of blaming God for results of our own choices, which is very pervasive in our culture.
2. **With self**, which changed from Adam and Eve having good self-esteem without any shame to covering their selves with leaves. That was the beginning of low self-esteem and mask wearing—pretending to be who we are not—not wanting others to see the transparent self.
3. **With the other gender**. Adam changed from bragging about Eve to blaming her (Genesis 3:12-13). That was the beginning of projecting problems on others, instead of accepting responsibility for one's own choices.
4. **With the environment**, which changed from cooperation with to competition against humans. From that point on humans would toil hard with fatigue and sweat when cultivating and harvesting food (Genesis 3:17-19). In fact, the cosmos was thrown off balance and into a dis-ease-ment. That is because God created this world with human righteousness upon which the cosmos would depend.

When the harmonious balance of human life was thrown into imbalance, the entire cosmos was affected. This is similar to what happens when one tire on a vehicle gets out of balance. It shakes the entire vehicle. Romans 8:19-21 reports the out-of-balance cosmos, "The creation waits in eager expectation for the sons of God to be revealed. For the creation was subjected to frustration, not by its own choice, but by the will of the one who subjected it, in hope that the creation itself will be liberated from its bondage to decay and brought into the glorious freedom of the children of God."

Their sin turned the community of unity in the garden into chaos of disunity

Expulsion from the Garden and Life Today

Adam and Eve were expelled from the garden so they would not be able to take from the tree of life and live on earth forever without God's Spirit. It seems that the tree of life provided the primary source for Adam and Eve to continuously live physically with their choices. Without God's inner source—His live-in Spirit—for proper relationships, people will adopt non-godly external sources for defining what is relationally right and wrong. To disregard God's way is to turn the perfect garden into a perverted hell on earth. To do that while continuously eating from the tree of life is to endlessly deepen the perversions. Consequently, God declared that mankind disregarding God, "must not be allowed to reach out his hand and take also from the tree of life and eat, and live forever" (Genesis 3:22. See the continuous availability of the tree of life in heaven in Revelation 2:7; 22:2, 14, 19). Thus God expelled Adam and Eve from the garden in order "to guard the way to the tree of life" (Genesis 3:24). Doing that insured that the present generation would eventually end and perhaps the next generation would improve life on earth. That is a way to put a check on the continuous spread of the cancer of evil.

After their sin (and ours), there is a remnant of God's likeness in people. If all people became totally depraved, God could not have said to Cain after he killed his brother, "If you do what is right, will you not be accepted? Sin is crouching at your door; it desires to have you, but you must master it" (Genesis 4:7). Today we see goodness from non-Christians, such as the rich caring for the poor; hospitals and shelters for abused women; new inventions that benefit people; research and breakthroughs in medicine; benevolence; neighbors helping neighbors after tragedies; search parties organized for lost people; positive scientific contributions; writing and passing positive laws to protect people; positive contributions in literature, theater, education, music, art, government, and so on. God established government leaders to be His ministers in order to reward the good and punish the evil, and ordered Christians to submit to them. He surely would not have done that if these leaders were totally depraved (Romans 13:1-7). Why would Paul appeal to a totally depraved Caesar (Acts 25:11)?

After their sin (and ours) there is a remnant of God's likeness in people

Many of the above positive contributions are linked to socialization; but socialization could not produce good results if all people are depraved from birth. Even pagan mothers could not love and care for their children. However, without God's Spirit, humans lose their freedom to consistently apply God's love that represents and reflects Him. Disconnection from God's live-in Spirit will gradually motivate individuals from living with "**inter**dependence with God and each other to living with total **in**dependence from Him and each other—a weakened and sick excuse for community. As people become addicted to independence, the good from science, medicine, theater, laws, etc., becomes not good. We are being unrealistic not to notice the gradual cultural changes from the 1950's to the present, such as the increase in inhumane violence, vulgarity, pornography in theater, abortions, transsexual surgery; the legal changes that protect irresponsible freedom of speech; homosexuality; the changes in movies, television, entertainment, literature, and so on.

Disconnection from God's live-in Spirit will gradually motivate individuals from living with interdependence with God and each other to living with total independence from Him and each other—a weakened and sick excuse for community

The "Godufactured" Shattered

Without God's Spirit permeating a culture through individuals living in accordance with His inner Spirit, a culture will turn from prioritizing interdependence to independence; from looking upward to looking inward; from serving others to serving only self; from preserving life to taking life; from honoring deity to deifying what is not divine; from wanting to fulfill God's will to working to fulfill only our wants and wishes; from generosity to greed; from cooperation to competition; from loving to loathing; from looking out for others to primarily looking out for self; from the majority respecting and protecting the rights and needs of the minority to reducing their rights and neglecting their needs; from dedication to community to destruction of community; from living with faith in God to faith in gadgets; from protecting life to destroying it; from focusing on the *Elohim* to focusing on the Ego; and so on.

As the perceived "superior" segments of society purposely neglects the rights and needs of the perceived "inferior" segments, such as the rich neglecting the poor; whites neglecting blacks; the educated excluding the uneducated; males marginalizing females; citizens abusing immigrants; homeowners belittling homeless, and so on community will be replaced by chaos, and cooperation by competition and conflict. Nowhere has this been more obvious in the history of the United States than during the Civil War.

While the national North/South Civil War is over, minor civil wars continue in all kinds of relationships, such as union workers with non-union workers; Republicans with Democrats; rich with poor; CEOs with the lowest wage earners; blacks with whites; males with females; one Christian denomination with other Christian denominations. Christians with non-Christians; one sibling with another sibling over such things as the family inheritance, and so on.

Cain waged that kind of minor civil war against Abel; however, no civil war is minor to either the losers who are imminently hurt or the winners who do the hurting. Cain replaced respect for his brother with revenge, and cooperation with Abel with competition that led to conflict. Their family community was weakened. Lack of family community weakens neighborhood community. Lack of neighborhood community weakens city community. Lack of city community weakens county community. Lack of county community weakens state community. Lack of state community weakens national community. Lack of national community weakens world community. What we do individually eventually affects others in a scope beyond our imagination.

We do not know how long it took, but at some point in time the holistic lack of community was described, "The Lord saw how great man's wickedness on the earth had become, and that every inclination of the thoughts of his heart was only evil all the time (Genesis 6:5). That means every motivation of anyone's decisions was damaging to others and self.

If life were like that today, we could not do anything with any peace or security. We could not eat food prepared by another, because of the evil intentions of the preparers. We could not purchase packaged or canned food, because of the evil motivations of the packers. We could not fly on a plane, because of the mean intentions of the pilot, air traffic controllers, and passengers. We could not drive through a green light, because of the evil plans of those who program the sequence of the lights, and so on. There is not a single thing we could do without stress, frustration, and harmful results. The kind of world that evolved was summarized with, "Now the earth was corrupt in God's sight and was full of violence" (Genesis 6:11).

No wonder God "was grieved that he had made man on the earth, and his heart was filled with pain" (Genesis 6:6). There were several ways God could have responded, such as to leave the situation alone and watch people destroy each other; eliminate all human life to let the planet decay to its previous formlessness and emptiness, or eliminate some people, but keep a few for a fresh start.

While the national North/South Civil War is over, minor civil wars continue in all kinds of relationships

We will turn to God's decision and the aftermath of it in the next chapter.

4

God's Preparation For The Restoration of Humanity

God's Grace for our Disgrace

As soon as Adam and Eve "missed the mark" (sinned), God revealed unfailing love by promising a future arrival of the Messiah to save people from the eternal consequences of sin, "And I will put enmity between you and the woman, and between your offspring and hers; he will crush your head, and you will strike his heel" (Genesis 3:15). God is the original Promise Keeper who will not let anything keep Him from fulfilling that promise.

When mankind's sin had reached the point of grieving God so much that He would no longer tolerate their evil, He did not choose to eliminate all human life on earth. Instead of the deluge revealing only punishment, His universal flood communicated His "showers of love" to stop the rapid spread of evil by starting over with a small remnant of eight people and a diversity of animals. But despite God's opportunity for a fresh start, dysfunctional living quickly resumed and spread as the population increased.

Eventually people united to build a tower to reach the heavens. However, their unity was not to please God, to worship God, to get closer to God, and to serve God; but rather selfishly, "Come, let **us** build **ourselves** a city, with a tower that reaches to the heavens, so that **we** may make a name for **ourselves** . . ." (Genesis 11:4; bold print added). They excluded God—even from asking His help to become more creative in doing quality construction.

God's Call to Privilege and Purpose

At some point in time God decided to develop a people to be His people. Although we know them as the Hebrew people (Israelites, Jews), that nationality did not exist at that time. The Jewish nation began with the call to one person. Later God reminded His people about their small beginning, "Listen to me, you who pursue righteousness and who seek the Lord: Look to the rock from which you were cut and to the quarry from which you were hewn; look to Abraham, your father, and to Sarah, who gave you birth. When I called him he was but one, and I blessed him and made him many" (Isaiah 51:1-2).

Abram lived in the geographical area now known as Iraq, which was polytheistic and filled with perverted morals and violence. But God saw potential in Abram if he would separate from that area; and thus selected Abram with the choice to "Leave your country, your people and your father's household and go to the land I will show you" (Genesis 12:1).

God was not being preferential by selecting Abram and thus his descendents. Instead of being preferential, God was purposely planning His beneficial ministry to all peoples by investing Himself in one people, and thus through them to and for all others. The heavenly Father shared with the Hebrew people His character, His teachings, His intentions, His direction, His discipline, His patience, His companionship, His loves, His hates, His inspiration, His angels, His Spirit, and eventually His Son—in summary Himself. By doing that, God equipped the Hebrew nation to be able to voluntarily represent Him with their lips and lives so others could know what He is like through them.

God issued a two-sided call to Abram—to privilege and to purpose. The privilege side included what God promised to do **for** Abram and his descendents, the Hebrew people. The purpose side included what God wanted to do **through** Abram and his descendents as reported in Genesis 12:2-3:

The Privilege:

> I will make you into a great nation,
> I will bless you;
> I will make your name great . . ..
> I will bless those who bless you,
> and whoever curses you I will curse;

The Purpose:

> and you will be a blessing . . ..
> and all peoples on earth will be blessed through you.

God equipped the Hebrew nation to be able to voluntarily represent Him with their lips and lives so others could know what He is like through them

Shaping the Hebrew people into a great nation included God's gifts (privileges) so they could be a blessing to others (purpose). But notice to which others—not just to themselves, but **all peoples on earth.**

God's strategy for blessing people has never changed. God's divine conspiracy against Satan is to bless all kinds of people through His people. No one is excluded from "all peoples on earth." However, individuals and specific groups of people will be left out if God's people are not open to those specific kinds including those in the following list:

> The top one percent of the richest.
> The bottom one percent of the poorest.
> All persons between those two one percents.
> Those who are physically well most of the time.
> Those who are sick most of the time.
> Those married to only one mate.

Those who are married to many mates at the same time.
Those married and divorced many times.
Those who are living together as lovers, but not married.
The heterosexuals.
The homosexuals.
The lesbians.
Those who are beauty contest winner kinds of people.
Those who are extremely ugly.
Those who are mentally handicapped.
Those who are physically handicapped.
Those who are black.
Those who are white (more accurately pinkish beige, since none is really "white").
Those with various shades of skin color.
Those who own winter and summer houses.
Those who are homeless.
The believers.
The atheists.
Those with graduate and post-graduate degrees.
Those who dropped out of elementary school.
Those who are literate and even authors.
Those who are illiterate and can't even draw pictures.
Those who live in the nicest neighborhoods.
Those who live in one-room shanties, underneath bridges, and along sidewalks.
Those who drive new cars and RVs.
Those who drive stolen vehicles.
Those who use only bicycles.
Those who do not even have bicycles.
Those who are child abusers.
Those who are mate abusers.
Those who have had abortions.
Those who perform abortions.
Those who have murdered others.
Those who live in third world countries.
Those who worship other gods.
Those who worship Satan.

Those who are prostitutes.
Those who are pimps.
Those who intentionally transmit AIDS to others.
Those who are drug dealers.
Those who harvest or manufacture drugs.
Those who are drug addicts.
Those who are sex offenders.
Those who steal from others with pen or pistol.
Those who are in prison.
Those who are ex-convicts.
Those who are day laborers.
Those who are managers and CEOs.
Those who will not work, because they are lazy.
Those who are workaholics.
Those who are alcoholics.

God's divine conspiracy against Satan is to bless all kinds of people through His people

Now study the above list to analyze which of those kinds would your congregation not want to include.

Privilege and Purpose Out of Balance

From the outset, God's people are to be **inclusively open to all.** However, through the centuries God's people stressed the privilege side of their call by teachings such as, "We are blessed; we have the right God; we have the right place to worship God; we have the right rituals to worship God; we have God's revelation and presence; we have God's blessings; we have God's forgiveness; we have God's right celebrations and festivals," and so on. It is certainly appropriate to emphasize God's privileges, to appreciate them, and to pass them on to the next generations, but not at the expense of neglecting God's purpose for those privileges.

Gradually God's people did not balance God's privileges to them with God's purpose through them. The Old Testament prophets spoke and wrote to motivate God's people primarily to get purpose—the way they relate to others—in sync with God's privileges to them as revealed in the following small sampling:

1. "Learn to do what is right, seek justice, encourage the oppressed. Defend the cause of the fatherless, plead the case of the widow" (Isaiah 1:17-18).
2. "It is too small a thing for you to be my servant to restore the tribes of Jacob and bring back those of Israel I have kept. I will also make you a light for the Gentiles, that you may bring my salvation to the ends of the earth" (Isaiah 49:6).
3. Jonah was so upset that God brought repentance to a Gentile city that He prayed to God to let him die (Jonah 4:3). To that God responded, "You have been concerned about this vine, though you did not tend it or make it grow. It sprang up overnight and died overnight. But Nineveh has more than a hundred and twenty thousand people who cannot tell their right hand from their left, and many cattle as well. Should I not be concerned about that great city" (Jonah 4:10-11)?
4. About God's people who cheated the poor, God said, "Am I still to forget, O wicked house, your ill-gotten treasures. . . .Shall I acquit a man with dishonest scales with a bag of false weights? Her rich men are violent; her people are liars and their tongues speak deceitfully"(Micah 6:10-12).
5. "Hear this word. . .you women who oppress the poor and crush the needy . . . you will be cast out" (Amos 4:1-3).
6. "You trample on the poor and force him to give you grain. . . .For I know how many are your offenses and how great your sins. You oppress the righteous and take bribes and you deprive the poor of justice in the courts" (Amos 5:11-12).
7. God revealed that He could not stand their worship services, would not accept their offerings, and would not listen to the "noise" of their songs until they stopped oppressing people and started letting "justice roll on like a river, righteousness like a never-falling stream" (Amos 5:21-24).
8. God sharply condemned His people for lounging on beds of ivory, feasting on choice lambs and fattened calves, being entertained by musicians while being complacent about the problems of people around them (Amos 6:1-7).

God's Preparation For The Restoration of Humanity

Gradually God's People did not balance God's privileges to them with God's purpose through them

God's Law as Protection

In addition to calling a people, God shared His guidance as a protection for them. It may be surprising to realize that the Law was given first of all to protect His people from destroying themselves and others. There are 613 laws in the Old Testament; some deal with what to do, and some with what not to do. But all are relational. There is not one law that does not deal with how to relate properly to either God, self, others, or things. Each one expresses how to how live in love relationships. Seven times God's leaders identified the Old Testament as the "covenant of love" (Deuteronomy 7:9, 12; 1 Kings 8:23; 2 Chronicles 6:14; Nehemiah 1:5; 9:32; Daniel 9:4). To love exactly as God loves is one way to measure how close we are to being conformed to the likeness of God.

The law system is like having guardrails on a winding mountain road; each law is like a portion of the guardrails along the hi-ways of life. As long as people remain inside the "rails," they will not destroy one another or be destroyed. In order to help keep them inside that protection, God coupled the law with extrinsic motivations of punishment if the laws were disobeyed, and rewards if they were obeyed. That kind of discipline did not come from a hateful heavenly Father, but from a loving one as described in the book of Hebrews, "My son, do not make light of the Lord's discipline, and do not lose heart when he rebukes you, because the Lord disciplines those he loves, and he punishes everyone he accepts as a son" (Hebrews 12:5-6).

God's Law as Preparation

Beyond the immediate purpose of the law for protecting and guiding the Hebrew people, God's ultimate purpose of the law was to prepare His people to recognize and embrace pure love when it would arrive in the person of God's Son, and to confess their faith in Him. Paul explained,

"Now before faith came, we were imprisoned and guarded under the law until faith would be revealed. Therefore the law was our disciplinarian until Christ came, so that we might be justified by faith" (Galatians 3:23-24, NRSV). Where the New Revised Standard Version translates the Greek word *paidagogos* as "disciplinarian", The New International Version translates it as "tutor", and the New American Standard translates it as "to lead us to" with the more correct translation in the footnote, "child-conductor." The Greek word described a domestic servant who escorted (conducted) the household children to the right schoolmaster. When the children connected with the correct teacher, that specific responsibility of the *paidagogos* was over. Our English words "pedagogue" (schoolteacher) and "pedagogy" (the function and work of a teacher) come directly from the Greek word used to describe the nature and function of the law system.

Biblically, the Hebrew people remained as "children", as it were, until Christ came to implant His Spirit in those who would accept Him as the Messiah and would commit their faith to him, which would enable them to mature into spiritual adulthood.

Renewal of the Holy Spirit Promised

In addition to preparing for the restoration of humanity by choosing and calling a people to be His people, and by creating the "guardrails" of the law, God promised to give the Holy Spirit, "I will give you a new heart and put a new spirit in you; I will remove from you your heart of stone and give you a heart of flesh. And I will put my Spirit in you and move you to follow my decrees. . ." (Ezekiel 36:26-27); and "I will put my Spirit in you and you will live. . ." (Ezekiel 37:14); and "I will pour out my Spirit on your offspring, and my blessing on your descendants" (Isaiah 44:3); and "I will pour out my Spirit on all people. Your sons and daughters will prophesy, your old men will dream dreams, your young men will see visions. Even on my servants, both men and women, I will pour out my Spirit in those days" (Joel 2:28-29).

This promise was initially fulfilled with the creation of the Church as declared by Peter in Acts 2:17-18. According to the New Covenant, the Holy Spirit continues to be renewed in and for God's people, "Repent and be baptized, every one of you, in the name of Jesus Christ for the forgiveness of your sins. And you will receive the gift of the Holy Spirit. The promise is for you and your children and for all who are far off" (Acts 2:38-39; see also such texts as Romans 8:9-17; Galatians 3:1-2; Titus 3:5).

While the law is accompanied with external motivations—punishments and rewards—for doing or not doing God's will, the Spirit provides intrinsic motivation—the indwelling presence of God who equips us with His own relational character that motivates us to want to do His will. With His Spirit we can again live in accordance with God's original created design to reflect His character (Genesis 1:26). "Therefore, if anyone is in Christ, he is a new creation; the old has gone, the new has come" (2 Corinthians 5:17). With the **privilege** of God's Spirit living in us, we can be living channels of His **purpose** to bless all kinds of people through us, "We are therefore Christ's ambassadors . . .. (2 Corinthians 5:20). But before that would happen, this planet would experience God's people misrepresenting His call, as we will see.

With God's Spirit we can again live in accordance with God's original created design to reflect His character

Reductionistic Living

God's people gradually rejected being a blessing to **all** people. They reduced "**all**" to only "**one**"—themselves. They even excluded many categories of people within Judaism from enjoying God's equal blessings.

Through the centuries Abraham's descendants began to label (stereotype, mark, codify, tag, catalogue, rank, and pigeonhole) people into certain groups. Then they devalued selected people within those groups, and excluded them from experiencing God's love and blessings. Below are some of the groups with the identity of the excluded ones.

1. **The ethnic group.** God's people saw only two ethnic groups among humanity—the Jews and the Gentiles. By the time Jesus came, God's people perceived Gentiles to be like animal kind of people,

and referred to them with animal identities such as dogs. Jewish leaders required their people to go through ritual cleansings after touching a Gentile or anything a Gentile had touched. Unless Gentiles denied their ethnicity by being converted to Judaism, they were not blessed, but blasted—kept outside the circle of experiencing God's unfailing love.

2. **The health group**. Many Rabbis taught that God punished people with disease. Even Jesus' disciples once asked Him, "Rabbi, who sinned, this man or his parents, that he was born blind?" (John 9:2) The sick were not blessed, but blasted—kept outside the circle of experiencing God's unfailing love.

3. **The occupational group**. Jewish people in certain occupations were not permitted to enter a synagogue. For instance, Jewish tax collectors and shepherds were not blessed but blasted—kept outside the circle of experiencing God's unfailing love.

4. **The economical group**—rich and poor. Many Jewish leaders taught that God punished habitually sinful people with poverty. One Rabbi wrote that on the Day of Atonement the poorest of the poor should be "quartered", because they are archenemies of God. In that day a person was "quartered" by tying the legs and arms to horses, and then slapping the horses. The poor were not blessed, but blasted—kept outside the circle of experiencing God's unfailing love.

5. **The gender group**—male and female. By the time Jesus came, women were looked down upon and oppressed in many different ways. Rabbinic views of women did not come from the Old Testament, but from various teachings of philosophers that penetrated Jewish theology. For instance, Hesiod (750 BC) taught that a man who trusts womankind trusts deceivers. Pythagoras (530 BC) taught that all men are superior to all women. Democritus (460-370 BC) taught that a woman is morally weaker than a man. Aristotle (384-322 BC) taught that a woman is an imperfect man—a deformed man as seen in conception, and in her weaker development; a woman has inferior reasoning capacity; cannot be wise; cannot be a philosopher; is irrational; is not capable of being virtuous without a man; is naturally inferior to a man; is less spiritual than a man; is more mischievous than a man; and is more void of shame or self-respect.

There were many more negative philosophical teachings about women that shaped the way Jewish leaders treated women. Every day a Jewish man prayed to God, "Thank you for not making me a Gentile, a slave, or a woman." Women were viewed as having less value than Gentiles and slaves. Rabbis taught that it was evil to teach a woman the law; prayer was uttered before a meal if three men were present, but women were not counted; women were not to eat with men; women were separated from men in the synagogue with a sheet hiding their presence. The list of how women were oppressed is nearly endless. Women were not blessed, but blasted—kept outside the circle of experiencing God's unfailing love.

6. **The age group**—young and old. The Roman Caesar passed an Empire-wide law that when a baby was born and the father did not name it, the baby was to be taken away from the mother and abandoned in the wilderness to die alone. It is possible that the Caesar exempted Jews from keeping this law; however, the empire-wide law affected the way some Jews viewed and treated children. Jesus spoke harshly to Jews about abusing little children, which revealed their perceived lack of value (Matthew 18:1-9). Even Jesus' apostles rebuked people for bringing little children to Jesus, to which He indignantly responded, "Let the little children come to me, and do not hinder them, for the kingdom of God belongs to such as these" (Mark 10:13-14).

God's people blasted many kinds, rather than blessed all kinds of people; excluded many kinds, rather than included all kinds; isolated themselves from many kinds, rather than involved themselves with all kinds; hated many kinds, rather than loved all kinds; and sorted many kinds rather than served all kinds. Thus they were not being fully human in an inhuman world. What was needed to turn that around?

To that we turn next.

5

The Global Need: God With Skin On It

The Visit from Heaven

During World War II military personnel were often sent overseas for the remainder of the war unless they were badly wounded or had flown a predetermined number of aviation missions. A soldier had been gone a long time when his wife asked their ten-year-old son what he would like for Christmas. The lad looked at his Dad's picture on a nearby table and responded, "The gift I really want is for Dad to step out of that frame and be here with us."

Dave Stone, the senior associate preaching minister for the Southeast Christian Church in Louisville, Kentucky, tells what happened one night during a fierce thunderstorm. His son woke up in his room crying. Dave yelled from his room, "What's wrong, son?" The son replied, "Dad, I'm scared!" Dave gave an assuring response, "No need to be scared, son, God will take care of you." The boy thought a minute or two and then wisely called back, "Dad, I know God will take care of me, but right now I need someone with skin on." Isn't that what we all need from time to time?

The Global Need: God With Skin On It

Someone from heaven with skin on is precisely what this globe needed two thousand years ago in the midst of dysfunctional relationships between men and women; rich and poor; well and sick; young and old; owners and slaves; Jews and Gentiles; leaders and followers; atheists and believers, and so on. From the first human sin, God promised to send someone who would stand between people and Satan to defeat Satan's mission of dividing people from one another and from God. God kept that promise alive through the subsequent centuries.

God provided specific ways people would be able to recognize that person by prophesying in advance minute details of His life. Such prophecies include how He would be conceived, where He would be born, where He would be taken as a small lad for safety, what He would be called, the kinds of people He would help, the kinds of ministries He would do, an Elijah-like person would announce His imminent arrival, details about His execution (such as He would be pierced, would thirst, no bone would be broken), would not decay in the grave, would be resurrected, and so on. Jewish scholars have identified over 400 prophesies about the Messiah, all of which Jesus fulfilled. Peter Stoner in *Science Speaks* reported that the probability one person could fulfill just 60 prophesies is one in 100,000,000,000,000,000. Harold Hatzler of the American Scientific Affiliation noted that Stoner's book was reviewed by the Affiliation, which concluded that his mathematical analysis was based upon the principles of probability that are thoroughly sound and used by scientists. Those who refuse to affirm the Messiahship of Jesus will need to decide upon what bases, rather than fulfilled prophesies, they would identify the Messiah.

Someone from heaven with skin on is precisely what this globe needed

Divinity Among Us

Because humans were not living like God in their relationships, God decided to come to earth to live like a human through His relationships. John recorded the earthly visit of God with skin on, "In the beginning was the Word, and the Word was with God, and the Word was God. He was with God in the beginning" (John 1:1).

Logos, the Greek for "word", was used to communicate something that had significant meaning. John's Gospel began by reminding us that God had always disclosed Himself from the beginning. God communicated His eternal characteristics in numerous and diverse ways, which include being powerful, moral, loving, faithful, gracious, merciful, creative, eternal, patient, gentle, forgiving, and so on. Even the design and organization of this universe reveal aspects of God's nature as revealed in Psalm 19:1-4, "The heavens declare the glory of God; the skies proclaim the work of his hands. Day after day they pour forth speech; night after night they display knowledge. There is no speech or language where their voice is not heard." Paul reminded the skeptics of that truth when he wrote, "For since the creation of the world God's invisible qualities—his eternal power and divine nature—have been clearly seen, being understood from what has been made, so that men are without excuse" (Romans 1:20).

This full-of-significant-meaning "Word" was personal. The "Word" cannot be disconnected from the source, because the "Word" is identical with the source, "the Word was God." What we hear from God squares with how God is. He and His "Word" are transparent—no pretensions, cover-ups, hidden agendas, or fantasies. God is never not God, and what aspects He reveals about Himself are very personal—His deeds and declarations; His perceptions and practices; His attitudes and actions; His agape and anger; His loves and loathes; His friendships and forgiveness; His commands and compassion; and so on.

Jesus' inner and outer characteristics were not only to serve us, but also to show us clearly the nature of God. That was needed because through the ages the people God chose to represent Him covered up His nature. Gadgets and gods, prejudices and priorities, traditions and non-truths became spiritual cataracts that blurred their 20/20 vision, and shielded God's authentic character from others. So God personally visited this planet.

Because humans were not living like God in their relationships, God decided to come to earth to live like a human through relationships

A Perfect Human with Us

From eternity to earth; from the world outside our world to the womb inside a woman; from the invisible to the visible; and from Spirit to skin, "The Word became flesh and made his dwelling among us" (John 1:14a). Through close-up encounters with Jesus people saw in Him the character of someone who was fully human in an inhuman world, "We have seen his glory, the glory of the One and Only, who came from the Father" (John 1:14b). The word "glory" is from the Greek word *doxa*, which in those days referred to a person's character. Readers of the Bible would understand most texts better if *doxa* were translated "character" instead of "glory." People saw in Jesus' character the mirror of His Father in heaven, "full of grace and truth (John 1:14c).

Grace linked equally with truth is a tough balance to maintain. Grace refers to any activity of one person for the benefits of another. Truth refers to what squares with reality. A person can be full of one without the other. For instance, someone may give the shirt off his back, and even his back for another person in need (grace); however, he might be lacking in truth, and lead others to hell. On the other hand, someone may be full of truth, but might be lacking in grace. It is possible that some unbelievers think some Christians have a handle on truth, but cannot stand their attitudes with it.

> **People saw in Jesus' character the mirror of His Father in heaven and the model of being fully human in an inhuman world**

The One who lived a transparent life full of grace and truth was the Messiah God promised in Genesis 3:15, and prophesied with specifics throughout the Old Testament. Jesus, conceived in Nazareth and born in Bethlehem, continuously existed from eternity with the Father and the Holy Spirit as one of the three eternal members of the triune God.

Humanity and Divinity with Skin On

One text described Jesus this way, "Who, being in the **very nature** God did not consider equality with God something to be grasped, but made himself nothing, taking the **very nature** of a servant, being made in human likeness. And being found **in appearance** as a man, he humbled himself and became obedient to death—even death on a cross" (Philippians 2:6-8 Bold print mine).

Before Jesus was born, an Old Testament Prophet identified Him as, "God with us." (Matthew 1:23). Elsewhere He is identified as God (Hebrews 1:8;); the unique one-of-a-kind person with skin on (the Greek word *monogenes* in such places as John 3:16, 18); the image of the invisible God (Colossians 1:15); the radiance of God's glory [character] as the exact representation of God's being (Hebrews 1:3); the fullness of God (Colossians 1:19); the true God (1 John 5:20); the co-creator with the Father (John 1:2; Colossians 1:16); the immortal God (1 Timothy 6:14-16); the eternal God and eternal life (1 John 5:20). and the One "who is at the Father's side" (John 1:18). "At the Father's side" is literally " in the bosom of the Father" (KJV). To not translate it that way is to miss the cultural significance of that description. Jewish culture used the metaphor "in the bosom" of another to identify two beings who were in an authentic and holistic connection with each other. "In the bosom of the Father" was a culturally picturesque way to display Jesus' intimate and unbroken unity with the Father—the two who function as one.

Hang with me for a bit of in-depth teaching. Philippians 2:6-8 is a close-up snap-shot of that relationship. *Morphe* and *schema* are two Greek words in that section, which clearly expose the nature of Jesus. *Morphe* describes the essential internal nature of something, while *schema* describes the external packaging of the internal nature. Jesus was the "**very nature**" (*morphe*) of God, and took on the "**nature**" (*morphe*) of a servant. God has always been the servant-lord. The two cannot be disconnected, for both are aspects of God. However, when Jesus came to earth He came "**in appearance**" (*schema*) as a man—a human with skin on. That was the outer wrapping/packaging of His inner two-sided nature—God and servant. Since the Philippian text begins with "Your attitude should be the same as that of Christ Jesus" (verse 5), *morphe* and *schema* relate to our two-sided make-up as well. God originally created humans in his image and likeness as servants as He is—our *morphe*—side one of our make-up.

Our *schema,* the outer wrapping/packaging through which our essential nature—in the likeness of God, and as a servant—are expressed is identified with whatever, wherever, and however we are serving through our private and public actions such as in careers, families, leisure activities, and so on—side two of our make-up. God has always been a servant and the leader—a servant-leader (his essential nature), and so should we. Everyone is a leader to someone. But what kind of leader, and for what reason?

Jesus as God's Show and Tell

Why did Good package Jesus' essential nature inside human skin? He did it to be heaven's show and tell on earth. Most Jews and Gentiles harbored badly distorted perceptions of God's character. Many thought God was a narrow legalist with prejudices against most people, as One who neglected people, held grudges, and oppressed people. Many thought God's nature was characterized more by anger than agape; by more fault-finding than forgiving; by being more grabby than gracious; by being more rich in materials than righteous in manners; by being more exclusive than inclusive; by being more punitive than peaceful; by being more hostile than harmonious; by being more a foe than a friend; by being more legalistic than "lovalistic"; by being more ritual than relational; by being more a respecter of persons than a redeemer of persons; by being more distant than near; by being more interested in revenge than in reconciliation; by being more closed than open; and by being more full of correction to others, than of compassion for them.

Because no one was holistically acquainted with the authentic and holistic nature of God, Jesus "made God known" (John 1:18, NIV). Other translations state Jesus' disclosure of God's nature differently, such as making God known "plain as day" (The Message); "unfolded" God (Moffatt); "told us all about" God (The Living Bible); and "has shown us what God is like" (Contemporary English Version). Each translation communicates the same truth, which is that God was His own exegesis. Through Jesus' life, death, and resurrection, God "bill boarded" His invisible internal relational character. John wrote, "No one has ever seen God" (John 1:18a). However, Jesus later declared, "I and my Father are one" (John 10:30); and "Anyone who has seen me has seen the Father" (John 14:9).

God is Like Jesus

Anyone who wants to know what God is like needs to go no farther than to walk with Jesus through Matthew, Mark, Luke, and John; accompany Him in situations He encountered; notice whom He loved and how; observe how and why He served; listen to what He said; watch Him voluntarily die for the sins of others; and grasp His eternality through His resurrection.

How did Jesus show us what God is like? He did it by what He declared verbally and demonstrated relationally. His was a minister of relationships—of "lovalism" not legalism. He revealed the nature of His ministry to His hometown synagogue by announcing that He was anointed to fulfill the prophecy of Isaiah 61:1-2, "The Spirit of the Lord is on me, because he has anointed me to preach good news to the poor. He has sent me to proclaim freedom for the prisoners and recovery of sight for the blind, to release the oppressed, to proclaim the year of the Lord's favor" (Luke 4:18-19). The poor referred not only to those who were spiritually poor, but also to the materially poor; prisoners referred not only to criminals, but also to those imprisoned by a dysfunctional lifestyle; the blind referred not only to the spiritually blind, but also to the physically blind as representing anyone with a disease; the oppressed referred not only to those being oppressed by the devil, but also to those held down by religious and cultural prejudices.

His hometown friends heard that Jesus was committed to love those they hated to love; touch the untouchables; help the helpless; befriend the friendless; welcome the unwanted; free the fettered; partner with the poor; involve the incarcerated; and bring optimism to the oppressed. By relating to those kinds, Jesus challenged the prejudices and hatreds fed not only by secular leaders and followers, but also by religious leaders and followers. When His hometown folks heard this, they tried to kill Him—the first recorded attempt to eliminate the earthly visit of God with skin on. (Luke 4:28-30).

However, that did not distract Jesus from doing what He came to do—to be a relational show and tell of God. He did not just tell a leper he would be healed, but also did the unacceptable—He touched him. God is like that, and so should we be. He stood alone with a woman caught in adultery and forgave her. God is like that, and so should we be. He allowed a well-known sinful woman to touch him, wet his feet with her tears, and wipe them with her hair, which was a dynamic demonstration of His acceptance of her value. God is like that, and so should we be. He helped a non-Jewish widow; gave a new lease on life to a woman who had been married five times and was living with a man to whom she was not married. God is like that, and so should we be. He allowed women to tell men the good news that He had risen. God is like that, and so should we be. He invited some of the most unlikely to be His partners and to expand His ministry. God is like that, and so should we be. He bragged about the generosity of a very poor widow. God is like that, and so should we be. He criticized religious leaders for prioritizing rituals and traditions above helping hurting people. God is like that, and so should we be. On the cross He saved a criminal others despised. God is like that, and so should we be, and He refused to be controlled by religious leaders who were hooked on non-biblical traditions. God is like that, and so should we be. **God modeled through Jesus what it means to be fully human in an inhuman world.**

Jesus committed Himself to love those others hated to love

Through Jesus' actions and reactions we know that God is willing to leave the crowd to search for only one lost person, and so should we. He is interruptible and approachable, and so should we. He waits for a rebellious son to return, runs, hugs, kisses, and restores him, and so should we. He buddies up with the poorest of the poor and the richest of the rich, and so should we. He cares for minor problems, such as a fever and major problems, such as leprosy, and so should we. He takes time to wash feet and feed thousands, and so should we. He is comfortable talking and walking with both little known and well-known people, and so should we. He pays taxes to the government, and so should we. He goes the second mile to help someone, and so should we. He forgives whatever a person has done, and so should we. And He offers eternal life to everyone, and so should we.

To relate the way Jesus related is one way to measure how close we are to being conformed to the likeness of God.

Jesus lived, worked, and ministered outside the box of traditional religion that was more interested in being correct than being compassionate; more interested in rituals than relationships; more concerned about tradition than truth; and more concerned about status than service. That same Jesus upsets some white people today who do not want, and may not tolerate, a black person sitting next them in worship; a homeless person being baptized in the same water as the bank President; a woman reading the Bible and praying from the podium with men present; people who have had an abortion working in the children's department; an ex convict becoming a leader in the church, and so on. Is it possible that our personal perceptions and prejudices shape our commitments to authentic Christianity more than the practices and priorities modeled by Jesus, the Head of His on-going body, the Church? No wonder Paul wrote that all Christians are to "reach unity in the faith and in the knowledge of the Son of God and become mature, attaining to the whole measure of the fullness of Christ" (Ephesians 4:13). Notice, Paul did not write that we are to reach unity in the faith and the knowledge of the end times, of the charismatic movement, of eternal security, of the frequency and mold of the Lord's Supper, and so on, but of Jesus—who He was, and how He was—so we can mature into His likeness.

Jesus for Today

It is as easy to miss what God is like in the twenty-first century as it was in the first century. God's character will certainly not be known, understood, appreciated, and valued, and applied without meeting God in Jesus. That requires becoming more acquainted with Jesus. Is it possible that Church leaders today assume people know all about Jesus, so other topics get more teaching and preaching than Jesus? Is it possible that we put Jesus on the back burner, because as His ways were too relationally liberal in His day, they still are in our day? He called people to follow Him, and that invitation continues. But we cannot intentionally follow whom we do not know. Instead of following Him, we might want to eliminate Him in order to get on with our traditions, as many did in His day.

Jesus' life applied God's first call to His people, "all peoples on earth will be blessed through you" (Genesis 12:3). In actualizing that call, Jesus made is crystal clear that God is relational. God knows all about us, likes, and loves us in spite of what He knows about us, and wants everyone to be re-connected to Him through Jesus. Without one slight whimper or waver, Jesus consistently lived God's own relational ministry, which He explained, "I tell you the truth, the Son can do nothing by himself; he can do only what he sees his Father doing, because whatever the Father does the Son also does" (John 5:19). ". . .I do nothing on my own but speak just what the Father has taught me" (John 8:28). "For I did not speak of my own accord, but the Father who sent me commanded me what to say and how to say it" (John 12:49). He spoke and served to please the Father by blessing those who had been blasted by secular perversions and by religious traditions. And by doing that demonstrated, "God is like this!" Here is a sampling of what God was like then, still is today, and what it means to be fully human in an inhuman world.

1. Included both women and men to be His students. God is like that, and so should we be.
2. Welcomed both children and adults. God is like that, and so should we be.
3. Included an exploiter of peoples' money as one of His apostles, the tax collector Matthew, and invited him to live differently. God is like that, and so should we be.
4. Touched the ritually and socially unclean. God is like that, and so should we be.
5. Bragged about a person whose ethnic identity the religious leaders hated—a Samaritan. God is like that, and so should we be.
6. Had a reputation for being a friend of sinners. God is like that, and so should we be.
7. Forgave sins of all kinds, except blasphemy against the Holy Spirit. God is like that, and so should we be.
8. Looked at the crowds filled with dysfunctional people and had compassion for them. God is like that, and so should we be.
9. Linked service to His leadership and humility to His status. God is like that, and so should we be.
10. Valued people above property. God is like that, and so should we be.

11. Honored giving away riches above having and keeping them. God is like that, and so should we be.

Jesus erased all kinds of labels that stereotyped people to keep them "in their places." By doing that, Jesus put flesh and bones—head, heart, hands, and feelings to God's love for all, "For God so loved the world that he gave his one and only Son, that whoever believes in him shall not perish but have eternal life. For God did not send his son into the world to condemn the world, but to save the world through him. Whoever believes in him is not condemned, but whoever does not believe stands condemned already because he has not believed in the name of God's one and only Son. This is the verdict, Light has come into the world, but men loved darkness instead of light . . . But whoever lives by the truth comes into the light, so that it may be seen plainly that what he has done has been done through God" (John 3:16-21).

Jesus modeled how to be fully human in an inhuman world

Therefore, Jesus not only revealed what God is like, but also what people created in God's image are to be like. He modeled how to be fully human in an inhuman world. Jesus also introduced God's ultimate purpose of restoring all categories of people to His original desire and design, for He came to seek and to save the lost (Luke 19:10). He offered His life, His death, His resurrection, and His Spirit for the restoration of humanity to God, "I am the way and the truth and the life. No one comes to the Father except through me" (John 14:6). But how can we be "Re-Godufactured" through Jesus?

To that we turn next.

6

Jesus: The Restoring God

There is a religious group that refers to itself as The Restoration Movement (Disciples of Christ, Christian Church, and Church of Christ). However, the original Restoration Movement was God's movement and ministry in Jesus for all humans.

Sin Disconnects from God

Humanity's separation from the intimate indwelling presence of God has never changed since God declared to Adam and Eve the result of sin— Death (Genesis 2:18; Isaiah 59:2; Ephesians 2:1-4). Paul affirmed that the wages of sin is still Death (Romans 6:23). The big "D" kind of death is the separational dis-ease-ment of mankind from God. " Therefore, just as sin entered the world through one man, and death through sin, and in this way death came to all men, **because all sinned**" (Romans 5:12. Bold mine). We continue what Adam and Eve did because of our choices, not theirs. If all of us inherited their sin, and thus their separation from God, the Psalmist would not have thanked God for wonderfully, skillfully and respectfully weaving him in his mother's womb, that he summarized it with, "your works are wonderful" (Psalm 139:13-15).

We are sinners because **we ourselves** sin and bear our own consequences as God declared, "For every living soul belongs to me, the father as well as the son—both alike belong to me. The soul who sins is the one who will die" (Ezekiel 18:4). And, "He will not die for his father's sin . . . .. The soul who sins is the one who will die. The son will not share the guilt of the father, nor will the father share the guilt of the son. The righteousness of the righteous man will be credited to him, and the wickedness of the wicked will be charged against him" (Ezekiel 18:17, 20).

Our Desires and Sin

The devil lures and entices us through our basic desires, such as hunger, thirst, to be loved, sex, security, and so on. All of those are God-given desires and are good in themselves. God's commandments function as guardrails to keep us on the right track. As long as we stay within the guardrails we have broad freedom for meeting those desires, such as eating different foods, but not with gluttony, which is beyond the guardrails; drink different liquids, but not with drunkenness, which is beyond the guardrails; engaging in sex, but not in homosexual acts, and in heterosexual acts outside of marriage, which are beyond the guardrails. It is not wrong for a man and a woman to have physical desires for each other because of their authentic love for each other, but those desires are not to be actuated outside the box of marriage. (Who plans marrying the other one without those kinds of desires?).

Although the devil is like a roaring lion who is trying to devour us (1 Peter 5:8), we can resist his temptations while being thankful to God for having God-given desires. God will not allow us to be tempted beyond our level of spiritual maturity to handle them (1 Corinthians 10:13). However, we need to keep our eyes on the narrow road (Matthew 7:14) and maneuver past attractive exits to tempting side roads to not play with temptations. God's promise to not allow us to be tempted beyond what we can manage is balanced with our responsibility to resist the devil (James 4:7). We are to nip the temptation in the bud as commanded by Jesus with his figurative language of gouging out the eye and cutting off the hand (Matthew 5:27-30).

God will not allow us to be tempted beyond our level of spiritual maturity to handle them

As fully human, Jesus was tempted every way as we are, which included a broad diversity of desires, but without sinning (Hebrews 4:15). That is one reason we can come to Him to receive His help in our times of weakness (Hebrews 4:16). He helps us with His understanding and grace, because He experienced how attractive, alluring, and powerful temptations are, and how vulnerable we are.

Jesus' Disconnection from God for Us

Crucifixion was such a horrible execution that the Caesar passed a law that Roman citizens could not be crucified regardless of the crime they committed. Jesus accepted the worst kind of execution for the worst kinds of criminals. He voluntarily took our sins and crimes into His body as His own (1 Peter 2:22-24). He who had committed no sin became sin on that cross (2 Corinthians 5:21).

Hundreds of years before it happened, God inspired Isaiah to write about the certainty of it as if it had already happened.

> He was despised and rejected by men, a man of sorrows, and familiar with Suffering.... Surely he took up our infirmities and carried our sorrows, yet we considered him stricken by God, smitten by him, and afflicted. But he was pierced for our transgressions, he was crushed for our iniquities: the punishment that brought us peace was upon him, and by his wounds we were healed. We all, like sheep, have gone astray, each of us has turned to his own way; and the Lord has laid on him the iniquity of us all.... Yet it was the Lord's will to crush him and cause him to suffer, and though the Lord makes his life a guilt offering, he will see his offspring and prolong his days, and the will of the Lord will prosper in his hand (Isaiah 53:3-10).

He not only took the sins of humanity as His, but also the guilt for them (10), such as the guilt of killing over six million Jews when He took Hitler's holocaust as His own. He took the guilt of Jeffrey Dahmer who committed homosexual acts with teenage boys, killed them, cooked some of them, and ate their cooked meat. He took the guilt of Ted Bundy who picked up, had sex with, and killed women. He took the guilt of slipping into a little girl's bedroom at night, kidnapping her, raping her, and killing her. And that's not all. He took your small and large sins to the cross with Him, and declared to the world's judge, "Guilty! I myself am guilty!" As God poured our sins into Jesus' body, the Holy Spirit abandoned Him. As that happened, He absorbed our disconnection from the Father. He experienced the big "D" death we deserved—separation from God. That's why He shouted, "My God, my God, why have you forsaken me?" (Matthew 27:46). When He breathed His last breath with our sins inside Him, and without God's Spirit inside Him, He took our place in hell. For anyone who dies physically (small "d" death) without God's Spirit experiences the big "D" death—"shut out from the presence of God and the majesty of His power (2 Thessalonians 1:9).

Although He graciously took our sins as His, He will not take them from us without our permission, thus forcing us to live in heaven with Him if we do not choose to do so. Staying on the cross until He experienced the big "D" death communicated His desire for us to receive what He offered on the cross—His eternal life for the wages of our sins (Romans 6:23). We are saved from our sins by His love and grace, which we voluntarily receive through faith (Ephesians 2:8). That gift can be accepted or rejected; He will not violate our choice.

Jesus not only took all the sins of humanity as His, but also the guilt for them

Was Jesus forced to do it? Of course not! He said, " I lay down my life . . .No one takes it from me, but I lay it down of my own accord" (John 10:14-18). He could have called more than 72,000 angels (more than twelve legions) to stop it, but He did not (Matthew 26:53). Out of His, and the Father's love and grace for us, Jesus tasted the big "D" Death due us, and thus digested it as His (Hebrews 2:9). He did not take our physical death from us, for the mortality rate for us all is 100% unless Christ returns first. But He took away "the second death" (Revelation 20:14)—the big "D" one—separation from the Father.

Jesus: Our Redeemer

How do we know with certainty that Jesus did not die for some secret sins of His own? We know, because of what happened after His death on the cross, which was also prophesied by Isaiah, "After the suffering of his soul, he will see the light of life, and be satisfied (Isaiah 53:11). The "light of life" is a reference to the resurrection, which Jesus declared was the essential and indisputable sign of His Messiahship (Matthew 12:38-39).

Peter graphically reported the significance of the resurrection on the day of Pentecost when he reminded his hearers that although they put Jesus to death, God raised Him from the dead by freeing him from the "agony" of death, because "it was impossible for death to keep its hold on him" (Acts 2:23-24). The Greek word for "agony" is *odin*, which was not used anywhere else in the New Testament. However, it was a word used in other Greek literature to refer to birth pangs (as noted in the margin of the NASB and so translated in various versions). The pangs in a woman are evidence that life is in her womb, not death. And so it was in the tomb.

> **The gift can be accepted or rejected.
> He will not violate our choice**

Jesus' Resurrection and Our Forgiveness

The Holy Spirit re-entered Jesus' body because all sins of all people were forgiven by Jesus taking their sins and punishment as His own. Big "D" Death and small "d" death were no longer in that tomb. The tomb was like a woman's womb pregnant with life—God's Spirit of Life. The tomb was pulsating with birth pangs nonverbally communicating, "I am alive, and I am coming out with God's Spirit of Life regardless of how many soldiers are on guard outside. I am alive, and I am coming out regardless how secure that tomb is sealed. I am alive, and I am coming out regardless of how many people who cried, 'Crucify Him' are still in Jerusalem." We can imagine that His pangs continued in close proximity—three minutes apart; then two; then one; then 30 seconds; then the count down to zero; and then UP FROM THE GRAVE HE AROSE.

Because the wages of anyone's sin is Death (separation from God), Christ's resurrection is proof that Jesus had no sins of His own. Thus our sins are forgiven in Him who ransomed us from the condemnation of the big "D" Death. Paul reviewed that dynamic, "And if the Spirit of him who raised Jesus from the dead is living in you, he who raised Christ from the dead will also give life to your mortal bodies through his Spirit who lives in you" (Romans 8:11).

The Apostles' Creed captures the Jesus event well:

I believe in God the Father Almighty, Maker of heaven and earth. And in Jesus Christ His only Son our Lord; who was conceived by the Holy Ghost, born of the Virgin Mary, suffered under Pontius Pilate, was crucified, dead, and buried; he descended into hell; the third day he rose again from the dead; He ascended into heaven, and sitteth on the right hand of God, the Father Almighty; from thence he shall come to judge the quick and the dead. I believe in the Holy Ghost, the holy catholic Church, the communion of saints; the forgiveness of sins; the resurrection of the body; and the life everlasting. Amen.

Our "Re-Godufactured" Connection to God

Although all sins of all people are forgiven in Jesus' execution, God will not force anyone to receive that forgiveness. It is a free gift for voluntary acceptance. It is not a gift forced on us.

A gift requires both a giver and a receiver. But the receiver needs to know about the gift, believe it is offered, desire to have it, and then do what is required to receive it. To do what is required is not a work for earning it, but steps for receiving it. For instance, if someone were to deposit a gift of one million dollars in the bank for us, we would not be able to enjoy it if we never knew it existed. That's what evangelism is about—letting others know about the deposited gift of forgiveness. But if we knew about the gift in the bank, but did nothing required to obtain it, such as showing a notarized identity with a corresponding picture; signing the withdrawal slip; waiting a few days for the signature to be verified; and then coming to the bank to receive it or to transfer it; we would also not enjoy the gift deposited in our name. By doing the above, we would not be working to earn the gift, but only taking the necessary steps to accept it.

So it is with receiving God's gift of forgiveness. People need to know it is available. When Peter revealed the reality of the risen Jesus on the day the Church began, the first converts asked, "Brothers what shall we do?" (Acts 2:37). Peter did not say, "Wrong question. There is nothing you can do, because God has done it all. Forgiveness is yours now." They had already heard and believed Peter's good news that Jesus is the Messiah (Christ) God promised. So Peter replied, "Repent and be baptized, every one of you in the name of Jesus Christ for the forgiveness of your sins. And you shall receive the gift of the Holy Spirit" (Acts 2:38).

To repent means to "change the mind" about who Jesus is, and to turn away from sin. To be baptized means to be immersed in water, which is symbolically being buried with Christ into His big "D" Death in order that we will be raised with Him to a newness of His big "L" Life (Romans 6:2-14). We put on Christ through faith, repentance, and baptism (Galatians 3:26-27). As Christians, we are no longer living with just self, but also with Christ who lives in us through His Spirit (Galatians 2:20; Ephesians 2:22; 1 John 3:24).

It's For All

This gift is not available to only a few, but to everyone, "The promise is for you, and your children, and for all who are far off" (Acts 2:39). When Saul, the ring leader who tried to destroy Christianity, encountered Jesus on the road to Damascus, Saul asked the same question the first inquirers asked, "What shall I do, Lord?" (Acts 22:10a). Jesus did not say, "There is nothing to do, because God has done it all." He did not even say, "Just repeat this prayer after me and I will immediately take up residence in your heart." Instead, Jesus replied, "Now get up and go into the city, and you will be told what you must do" (Acts 9:6; see also 22:10b). Saul went into the city and waited to be told what to do. While waiting, he prayed and did not eat or drink anything for three days (Acts 9:9). Then Ananias came to Saul to communicate what Jesus required Saul to do, "And now what are you waiting for? Get up, be baptized and wash your sins away, calling on the name of the Lord" (Acts 22:16).

The person being baptized is doing no work at all, as a dead person is not working when being buried. Faith is not a passive word. It is a noun related to action, so much so that faith without a corresponding action is dead (James 2:26). While we do not do the works of the Jewish law, we are to do deeds of the royal law, which is love (James 2:8). To believe, repent, and be baptized is to be united to Jesus' big "D" Death on the cross, so His spiritual Death becomes ours, because ours was transferred to Him. His eternal Life in the Spirit is then infused into us.

In this response we are vicariously crucified with Christ in order to victoriously live with Him and for Him (Romans 6:3-10). "Therefore, if anyone is in Christ, he is a new creation; the old has gone, the new has come" (2 Corinthians 5:17). Being a new creation takes us back to our original creation—in the image and likeness of God (Genesis 1:26). In Christ we are re-"Godufactured" to be fully human in an inhuman world as God's personal ambassadors (2 Corinthians 5:18-20). In Christ we are recreated according to His kind so we can relate according to His ways.

Being a new creation takes us back to our original creation in the image and likeness of God. In Christ we are "re-Godufactured" to become fully human in an inhuman world

"Re-Godufactured" as Our Rebirth

Jesus said to Nicodemus, "I tell you the truth, no one can see the kingdom of God unless he is born again" (John 3:3). The word "again" is from the Greek word, *anothen,* which had two different meanings: (1) A repeated time—the sequence, and (2) From above or from—the source. Every time Jesus used *anothen* He referred to heaven, the source (John 3:3. 7, 31; 19:11). Nicodemus thought Jesus meant a second physical birth, "How can a man be born when he is old? Surely he cannot enter a second time into his mother's womb to be born"—a sequence (John 3:4). But Jesus shifted Nicodemus' sequence understanding to understanding that the source is from above, "I tell you the truth that no one can enter the kingdom of God unless he is born of water and the Spirit. Flesh gives birth to flesh, but the Spirit give birth to spirit. You should not be surprised at my saying, 'You must be born **from above**" (John 3:6-7). The bold print is my translation of *anothen*, which is supported by the preceding statement that the Spirit gives birth to the spirit, and by Jesus' subsequent statement, "I speak of heavenly things" (John 3:12).

In another text, John revealed why conversion is referred to as a birth, "No one who is born of God will continue to sin . . ." (1 John 3:9a). The tense of the Greek verb "continue to sin" means to continuously sin. The Christian no longer lets sin be that person's ongoing lifestyle. Why not? "because God's seed remains in him; he cannot go continuously sinning, "because he has been born of God" (1 John 3:9b). The "birth" reality is tied to the "seed" reality. The Greek word translated "seed" is *sperma*, from which came our English word "sperm." God's *sperma* is His Holy Spirit as seen in the last verse in this chapter, "And this is how we know that he lives in us; we know it by the Spirit he gave us" (1 John 3:24).

To believe, repent, and be baptized is to be united to Jesus' big "D" Death on the cross. His spiritual Death becomes ours, and His eternal Life in the Spirit is then infused into us

What do we receive when we receive His Spirit, His *sperma*, His seed? We receive God's own character equipment, so we can relate holistically with God's relational fruit of the Spirit (Galatians 5:22-23). With the Holy Spirit dwelling in us we can "participate in the divine nature and escape the corruption in the world caused by evil desires" (2 Peter 1:4).

What is God's goal for us who have God's *sperma* living in us, and how does it relate to our original creation and to being fully human in an inhuman world?

We will look into that next.

7

God's Goal For Us All

God's Seed in Us

Anyone is instantly born from above when God plants His seed (*sperma*) in that person. But why does anyone plant a seed? We plant seeds so they will grow up, but grow up how? Grow up "according to their kinds" Ever hear of a farmer planting corn seeds expecting to get an apple orchard, or sunflower seeds expecting to get peaches? Of course not!

With His seed in us, God equipped us to grow up according to His kind, which takes us back to Genesis 1:26 (chapter one in this book). The same seed that conceived the earthly Jesus is in each person who is born from above. As a seed is planted to grow, Jesus also grew holistically "in wisdom and stature and in favor with God and man" (Luke 2:52).

God's Goal for Us

Ever wonder what the results of a survey would be if Christians were asked, "What is God's goal for you?" Perhaps many might answer with one word, "Heaven." However, God's goal for us is not to get to heaven. Heaven is

God's final destination for us, but not His goal for us living on earth. There is usually a difference between a destination and a goal. For instance, a newly married couple might choose Hawaii for the honeymoon, but that destination would surely not be the goal for that honeymoon. It would surely be one bummer of a honeymoon if the goal were only the destination.

God's goal for the earthly Jesus was not Nazareth, Bethlehem, nor any other location, but rather that He would mature in accordance with the seed in Him so people who encountered Him would know what God is like through Jesus' mature attitudes, actions, and reactions. Jesus' life and death demonstrated God's relational character to all kinds of people.

But what is God's goal for us who live amid the crud of earthly practices and who walk on the crust of earth's planet? Before Jesus came to this earth, God decided (predetermined) that His goal for us is "to be conformed to the likeness of His Son" (Romans 8:29).

The Good of Romans 8:28 and the Goal of 8:29

Paul tightly connected Romans 8:28 with 8:29, "And we know that God causes all things to work together for good to those who love God, to those who are called according to His purpose. **For** whom He foreknew, He also predestined to become conformed to the image of His Son . . ." (NASB, bold print mine).

We should not get bogged down with the words "foreknew" and "predestined." We all have a degree of foreknowledge. For instance, when you know another person well, you know ahead of time (foreknowledge) how that person will respond to something you say or do. Good examples are parents with their children and those who have been married a long time. We can also decide ahead of time the goal we wish to reach (predestine) and then do what is necessary to reach that predetermined goal. I demonstrated foreknowledge when I predestined the goal of airplanes I controlled during ten years as an air traffic controller. When planes were headed toward each other, by the use of radar I had foreknowledge there would be a mid-air collision without instructions to the pilots. Before I went to O'Hare airport I decided the goal for every plane I would control, which was to arrive at the airport safely. God knows ahead of time what will help us reach his predetermined goal that we be conformed to the likeness of His Son, Jesus.

Before Jesus came to earth, God decided that His goal for us is to be conformed to the likeness of His Son

The good mentioned in verse 28 is the goal mentioned in verse 29. Verse 28 is one of the most memorized verses among Christians, "And we know that God causes all things to work together for good to those who love God, to those who are called according to His purpose." However, it is easy to not realize that the promise in verse 28 is revealed in verse 29, "For whom He foreknew, He also predestined to become conformed to the image of His Son . . .." Verse 29 is cemented to verse 28 with the word "for", which identifies the "good" promised in verse 28.

Verse 28 is not suggesting that God makes all things happen. Allowing something to happen is not synonymous with making it happen, wanting it to happen, or rejoicing when it happens. That text also does not suggest that every event, happening, situation, conduct, and experience is good. Many are bad and can hurt us. And when they do, God grieves with us. He is close to the broken hearted (Psalm 34:18), and His heart is pained when events are painful and not as He intended (Genesis 6:6).

Sometimes the list of the not good seems endless, and can set us back temporarily with disappointment, discouragement, and distress. However, the promise of verse 28 is that God is able to bring good out of the bad, beauty out of the ugly, benefits out of the bitter, and magnificence out of the mess. Nothing can derail, detour, or distract God from working with us to reach His goal for us to be fully human in an inhuman world.

But what is the good that God works out of the bad for His people? The "good" is that whatever is thrown at us can help us advance toward being conformed to the likeness of Christ—to His character and conduct, to His perspectives and practices, to His compassion and competence, to His forgiveness and friendships, to His loves and likes, to His reasons and results: to His service and submission, to His helps and humility, and so on. Regardless of how bad or bitter, how horrible or hurtful, how distasteful or devastating, how wrong or woeful, how perverted or painful anything is that might happen to us, around us, or from us, God works in us and with us to help us become more like His Son, and thus be more fully human in an inhuman world.

With the partnership of God's Holy Spirit we can mature to think the way Christ thought, to feel the way He felt, to love the way He loved, to act and react the way He did, to please the Father the way He did—in short, to live the way He did and would if He were here on earth. And He is here on earth inside of us through God's *sperma*, His seed, His own Holy Spirit (Romans 8:9-10). Thus the church is called the body of Christ with each member being a cell in that body.

What is the good that God works out of the bad? The good is that whatever is thrown at us can help us advance toward being conformed to the likeness of Christ

It is not the independent events that happen to us, against us, or from us that help us grow into the likeness of Christ, but it is the seed of God in us that responds to those happenings. For "It is God who works in you to will and to act according to his good purpose" (Philippians 2:13).

Maturing toward becoming like Christ is not only the rationale for Romans 8:28, but also the reason for the promises of 8:31-39 –nothing can really be eternally against us (31); we will be blessed with God's generosity (32); we will be affirmed (33); Christ intercedes for us (34); nothing in all creation will separate us from the love of God (35); we will overwhelmingly conquer anything that hits us through Him who loves us (36-39). The "good" of verse 28 and the grace of verses 30-39 are focused on the reality that God will work with us to move us toward the goal of being conformed to the likeness of Christ in verse 29. Verse 28 and verses 30-39 are like two divine slices of eternal bread holding together the eternal meat of verse 29.

Partnering with God

However, we are responsible for cooperating with God by being open to grow up into Christ, and not just grow old with Him. Thus God inspired Paul to write, "Have this attitude in you which was also in Christ Jesus" (Philippians 2:5, NASB); "Do all things without grumbling or disputing" (Philippians 2:14, NASB); ". . . holding fast to the word of life" (Philippians 2:15, NASB); ". . . rejoice in the Lord" (Philippians 3:1, NASB); "Do not be conformed to this world, but be transformed by the renewing of your mind" (Romans 12:2, NASB).

Jesus gave His invitation, "Come to me, all you who are weary and burdened, and I will give you rest. Take my yoke upon you and learn from me, for I am gentle and humble in heart, and you shall find rest for your souls. For my yoke is easy and my load is light" (Matthew 11:28-30). The original word for "easy" referred to something that was tailor made to fit well. Tradition recorded that Jesus had a sign over His carpenter's bench that read, "My yokes fit well (easily)." It was reported that He would not make a yoke for a team of animals until He put His hands over each body, measured each muscle, and then carved out a yoke that was well fitted to that specific team so the load it would pull would be lighter. And He does that for us. His yokes are individually custom made according to our charismas, abilities, dispositions, levels of spirituality, and our holistic needs. When we slide into our side of the yoke with Him in the other side, the load is lighter to bear.

His yokes are individually custom made according to our charismas, abilities, dispositions, levels of spirituality, and holistic needs

Maturing from the Mess

But how can bad, ugly, bitter, and unkind events help mature us to become fully human in an inhuman world? Here are some examples of how having God's seed in us and being yoked with the triune God might work for the good promised in verse 28 toward being more conformed to the Christlikeness of verse 29 that will in turn bring buoyant victory out of what looks like defeats in verses 30-39:

    1. The death of a loved one, such as a parent's child, which is one of the toughest tragedies any person experiences. Having lost his 20-year old daughter in a tragic auto mishap, this author can attest to the fact that grief will not be erased, but a person can live through it to become more like Christ in several ways such as the following: (A) To better understand how God felt by watching His Son being nailed to the cross. (B) To better accept our personal worth and value by knowing either God or Jesus could have stopped it, but did not. (C) To know that God traded the life of Jesus for all kinds of people, and that Jesus was willing to accept all sins as

His. That can better motivate us to value and treat others the way the Father and the Son do. (D) To be more supportive of evangelism and mission work around the world. (E) To start a grief recovery group in the church to support those who experience the death of loved ones. (F) To be better able to help another grieving person.

2. A significant financial loss, such as a stock market crash, loss of employment, destruction of property without sufficient insurance, loss of all retirement savings due to the bankruptcy of the company, and so on. How could those misfortunes help equip a person to become more like Christ? Following are some of those ways: (A) Living with less dependence upon materials and more upon the Master. (B) Not looking down on poor people who live in shanties or the homeless who curl up to sleep under cardboard boxes. (C) Creating or engaging in recovery groups to help jobless and financially strapped people. (D) Creating ways to help people obtain affordable housing. (E) Engaging in ministries for the homeless. (F) Realizing self worth is never measured by cash worth. (G) Being more willing to give away what we cannot keep (money and possessions) and to keep what we cannot lose—being more fully human living in an inhuman world.

3. A sin or crime personally committed that hurts others. God can work good out of that in the following ways: (A) Allowing us to really experience God's forgiving grace that we may have been taken for granted without intimately feeling it. (B) Extending grace and forgiveness to others. (C) Entering into an accountability group to help offenders (including self) not to repeat the sin or crime. (D) Developing ministries for those practicing dysfunctional lifestyles. (E) Being a shepherd kind of person for another.

4. Abandoned by close friends. How can God work something good out of that hurt? (A) Better understand Christ's emotional pain when all His apostles abandoned Him on the night He was betrayed, but He did not desert them. (B) Not desert our friends if they might be caught in some kind of serious wrong. (C) Decide not to quit the church because we did not get our way. (D) Pray for instead of prey upon others who hurt us. (E) Not get even, but forgive.

5. A convict living in prison. How can God work good out of that? (A) Get involved in prayer meetings and worship while in prison. (B) Read through the Bible several times while doing time. (C) Evangelize

other prisoners. (D) Get involved with Chuck Colson's Prison Ministry. And when released from prison: (A) Create or engage practical ways to serve those in prison and ex-prisoners. (B) Start a jail/prison ministry. (C) Encouraging the church to participate in a prison ministry. (D) Hire ex-prisoners.

God for Us and The Devil Against Us

There is no event or experience out of which God cannot work good for us, although the event or experience itself may be bad and bitter. The good is that experiences can help shape us to become more fully human living in an inhuman world as we live more the way Christ lived. However, being shaped to live more like Christ does not automatically happen because of those events and experiences.

The devil has many friends he can and does enlist to keep us from drawing closer to God and one another. Some think the devil is alive and well, but that is not true. He is alive, but not well. He is sick with a terminal dis-ease. And he wants to infect us with his dis-ease-ment so we will become more distant from the Father, His Son, and His Spirit. The devil wants us to be drunk with wine rather than be filled with God's Spirit. What God can use to draw us nearer to Him and others, the devil can use to pull us away from God and others. The devil will even use God's own words as He did with Adam and Eve (Genesis 3:1-5). And he will certainly use words of other people, as well as what they do. He will certainly use what we have just listed—loss of a loved one, financial loss, personal sins, being forsaken by friends, and being imprisoned for a crime.

The devil is also into conforming us, as is God. The difference is that the devil wants us to be conformed to his ways and to sinful slices of our external culture, while God wants us to be conformed to the internal culture of His seed, His Holy Spirit, His Christ, and Him who resides in us to preside in us. Paul addressed that when he wrote, "I urge you therefore, brethren, by the mercies of God, to present your bodies a living and holy sacrifice, acceptable to God, which is your spiritual service of worship. And do not be conformed to this world, but be transformed by the renewing of your mind, that you may prove what the will of God is, that which is good and acceptable and perfect" (Romans 12:1-2, NASB). In the same vein, James wrote, "Submit therefore to God. Resist the devil and he will flee from you. Draw near to God and he will draw near to you. Cleanse your hands your sinners; and purify your hearts, you double minded" (James 4: 7-8, NASB).

Participating in God's divine nature takes commitment and energy. Peter confirmed that when he wrote that we can participate in God's divine nature (2 Peter 1:4), and immediately followed that statement with changes needed for growth:

> Now for this very reason also, applying all diligence, in your faith supply moral excellence, and in *your* moral excellence, knowledge; and in *your* knowledge, self-control, and in *your* self-control, perseverance, and in *your* perseverance, godliness; and in *your* godliness, brotherly kindness, and in *your* brotherly kindness, love. For if these *qualities* are yours and are increasing, they render you neither useless nor unfruitful in the true knowledge of our Lord Jesus Christ. For he who lacks these *qualities* is blind or short-sighted, having forgotten *his* purification from his former sins. Therefore, brethren, be all the more diligent to make certain about His calling and choosing you; for as long as you practice these things, you will never stumble; for in this way the entrance into the eternal kingdom of our Lord and Savior Jesus Christ will be abundantly supplied to you (5-11, NASB).

The devil is also into conforming us, as is God. The difference is that the devil wants us to be conformed to him and to sinful slices of our external culture, while God wants us to be conformed to the internal nature of His seed, His Holy Spirit, His Christ, and Him who resides in us to preside in us

What will it take to help us add these qualities, grow up to Christlikeness, and be fully human in an inhuman world?

To that we turn in the next chapters.

8

Needed: Spirit-Filled Leaders

New Babies and New Christians

Ever wonder why newly "born from above" people are called "infants in Christ" (1 Corinthians 3:1) and "new born babies" (1 Peter 2:2)? It is because becoming a Christian is the beginning of a growth process. Many of the needs of the spiritual newborn are similar to the needs of the physical newborn, such as the need for others to invest their time, attention, and value to care for, touch, prioritize, model, and love in diverse and costly ways. Neither the physical nor the spiritual newborn will mature relationally without others.

    A few years ago in Norco, California authorities discovered a six-year old girl who had been chained to her bed all her life. She lived six years without anyone talking with her, hugging, rocking, kissing, and regularly changing her diapers. When found, she was not able to speak one simple human word; the diameter of her arms was the size of a quarter; and she weighed less than 30 pounds. The medical specialist did not know whether or not she would ever be able to become a relational human being. She would need to be nurtured as a newly born infant—held, talked with, sang to, cuddled, rocked, changed regularly, etc. Eight years later she still could not talk, and the potential for catching up was lost. Around the same time, authorities in one of the eastern states found a 15-year-old boy who from birth had lived hidden away in the hen house with the chickens. Many of his physical needs were met on schedule, but without intimate relationship with humans. When discovered, he could not speak human words, but made the same sounds as chickens, and ate his food the same way chickens did. Both the six-year and the 15-year old were growing older without maturing into relational persons.

Growing Old Versus Growing Up

Newborn Christians can grow old over decades without relationally growing up toward God's goal of Christlikeness. Wouldn't it be odd for a Christian to enroll in college still drinking out of infant milk bottles? To grow old in Christ without growing up into Christ is a systemic malfunction in the church, which has reached epidemic proportions. We unintentionally keep too many people drinking from spiritual milk bottles.

It would not be difficult to trace the source of that neglect partly to Christian colleges and seminaries, which graduate potential leaders for the church without exposing them to a progressive spiritual development program with disciplines that are essential for spiritual maturity. Thus they have no clue how to develop programs for maturing members.

I entered the Air Force during the Korean conflict, but I would not have developed from being a civilian to being an effective military person had it not been for a military leader in boot camp; and subsequent leaders in the Air Force's technical school for control tower operators. Even after passing with flying colors the air traffic control courses, I still would not have developed as an accomplished controller without a mature leader in the first control tower to which I was assigned. With proper mentoring, I became a supervisor in a control tower in Korea; later the youngest supervisor in the Air Force's busiest control tower; and after discharge from the military, a senior FAA air traffic controller at the world's busiest airport, Chicago's O'Hare. As I needed leaders in the military and in the air traffic control career, so I need leaders to help me continue to mature in Christ, and so do all Christians.

To grow old in Christ without growing up into Christ is a systemic malfunction in the church, which has reached epidemic proportions

Jesus Helping Us

Jesus modeled a strategy for spiritually maturing others in His ministry. Before sacrificing Himself as Savior, He lived as a Shepherd for people who were as helpless as sheep without one (Matthew 9:35-36; 1 Peter 2:24). Jesus was more than just any shepherd. He was the good Shepherd (John 10:11). He also continues to function as our great Shepherd as revealed by the writer of Hebrews, "May the God of peace, who through the blood of the eternal covenant brought back from the dead our Lord Jesus that great Shepherd of the sheep, equip you with everything good for doing his will, and may he work in us what is pleasing to him through Jesus Christ to whom be glory for ever and ever. Amen" (Hebrews 13:20-21). When He returns to earth, He will return not only as Lord and Savior, but also as the Chief Shepherd, "And when the Chief Shepherd appears, you will receive the crown of glory that will never fade away" (1 Peter 5:4. See also Matthew 25:31-46).

When Jesus left earth for heaven, He did not abandon us to a shepherdless existence. He announced how He would transfer His character to us by first inviting people to enter into a sheep-to-shepherd kind of relationship, "Follow me" (Matthew 8:22; 9:9; 19:21; Mark1:17; 2:14; 8:34; 10:21). The "character goal" of that relationship is to become like Him as He mentioned in Luke 6:40, " . . .but everyone who is fully trained will be like his teacher." The "shepherd goal" of that relationship is that sheep eventually become also shepherds. Among His last words to Peter were, "Feed my lambs . . .Take care of my sheep . . .Feed my sheep . . .Follow me . . .You must follow me" (John 21:15-22). To "follow" is not just to linger behind Jesus, but also to live as the Shepherd lived. To do that calls for us also to model and to teach others in understandable ways. Jesus did not say, "fleece my sheep" or "feed the giraffes."

People Helping People

While we are not to dumb down God's ways and teachings, we are to apply them to the level of peoples' understanding, so newborn lambs can become mature sheep, who can then also shepherd others. Thus Jesus' parting words included, "Therefore go and make disciples of all nations, baptizing them in the name of the Father and of the Son and of the Holy Spirit, and teaching them to obey everything I have commanded you. And surely I am with you always, to the very end of the age" (Matthew 28:19-20). People need to be taught to obey in order be conformed to the likeness of Christ. Only then can the "shepherd to sheep" relationship develop other shepherds who will continue the "shepherd to sheep" relationship until Christ returns.

Jesus shepherded His apostle-sheep so they could become apostle-shepherds, and in turn could bring newborn lambs to maturity. That is the legacy and strategy Jesus left as recorded in Ephesians 4:7-13, "But to each one of us grace has been given as Christ apportioned it. . . . It was he who gave some to be prophets, some to be evangelists, and some to be pastors and teachers, to prepare God's people for works of service, so that the body of Christ may be built up until we all reach unity in the faith and in the knowledge of the Son of God and become mature, attaining to the whole measure of the fullness of Christ."

To shepherd others the way Jesus did is one way to measure how close we are to being conformed to the likeness of God, and thus becoming fully human in an inhuman world.

As the shepherd-leader of the Church, Christ gifted others to be shepherd-leaders. But why? To prepare God's people for works of service. Ministry does not belong to a few, but to all members of the Church. What is the purpose of every member eventually being engaged in ministry? It is so the body of Christ may be built up, "From him the whole body, joined and held together by every supporting ligament, grows and builds itself up in love, **as each part does its work**" (Ephesians 4:16, bold mine). How long is that to continue? It is to continue, "until we all reach unity in the faith and in the knowledge of the Son of God." Is it possible that we spend too much time equipping and teaching members about all sorts of important spiritual things, but without having a comprehensive understanding of and commitment to Christ's ways and words? What is the goal of bringing people to the holistic knowledge of the Son of God? It is for members to become mature. What does it mean to be "mature"? It means to attain "to the whole measure of the fullness of Christ." Then we can naturally "speak the truth in love" (Ephesians 4:15). **To speak the truth in love as Jesus did is one way to measure how close we are being conformed to the likeness of God, and thus becoming fully human in an inhuman world.**

Ministry does not belong to a few, but to all members of the Church

Those who teach that it is not possible to reach that level this side of heaven miss God's only strategy against Satan. One evidence of "a-likeness-of-Christ" maturity is outlined in the next two verses in Ephesians, "Then we will no longer be infants, tossed back and forth by the waves, and blown here and there by every wind of teaching and by the cunning and craftiness of men in their deceitful scheming."

No wonder early elders in the church were called shepherds, not cowboys (Acts 20:28). Peter reminded fellow elders that being overseers did not mean being lords over, but rather examples of care giving shepherds (1 Peter 5:1-4). Because Jesus' culture was dominated by agricultural and livestock farming, the shepherd motif was immediately understood, while it may not be understood well in today's industrial urban culture. Therefore, it is important to sense how some of a shepherd's responsibilities are linked to Jesus and Church leaders. Here are some characteristics from Psalm 23 and John 10:1-18:

Psalm 23

1. Takes care of needs (verse 1).
2. Rests the flock (2a).
3. Leads the flock (2b).
4. Provides deep, peaceful resources—quiet waters are deep and peaceful, but they also give the idea of safety by avoiding rushing flash floods that could carry them away (2c).

5. Restores people (3a).
6. Guides in proper relationships (3b).
7. Being companions during times of stress (4a).
8. Tracks and protects others (4b).
9. Provides security (5a).
10. Models goodness (6a).
11. Loves the sheep (6b).
12. Does not forsake the sheep (6c).

John 10

1. Knows the way to Christ (2).
2. Makes the way readily accessible to others (3a).
3. Knows people by name that are in his care, which means he knows their uniquenesses, character traits, needs, and situations (3b).
4. Models life for others to follow (4a).
5. Speaks to those in his care and is immediately recognized by them (4b).
6. Sacrifices for others (11).
7. Will not abandon others when times are difficult or threatening (12).
8. Values the life and safety of others above self (15).
9. Is not competitive against other shepherds or sheep (16).
10. Commits to unity (16).

To care for others the way the Lord does is one way to measure how close we are to being conformed to the likeness of God.

Spirit-filled People

Because the Church needs Spirit-filled people to model the kind of leadership, we need to consider what it means to be that kind of leader.

Paul wrote about being Spirit-filled, "Do not get drunk on wine, which leads to debauchery. Instead be filled with the Spirit" (Ephesians 5:18). What do wine and the Spirit have in common? As wine fills a person, it begins to control the life of that person until that person is totally under the influence of wine. Being filled with the Spirit is like that.

However, there is one big difference between being filled with wine and the Spirit. Every Christian already has ALL the Spirit living inside. We do not take on any additional amounts of the Spirit as a person does with wine. To be filled with the Spirit is to have the fullness of Christ (His character) living in us (Ephesians 1:22-23). The question is not, "Do I have all the Spirit?" but, "Does the Spirit have all of me? Are my attitudes and actions, reactions and relationships, desires and dreams, priorities and practices, speech and services, and so on in line with the Spirit's? Is my life manifesting the fruit of the Spirit listed in Galatians 5:22-23?" Paul put it this way, "Since we live by the Spirit, let us keep in step with the Spirit" (Galatians 5:25). Living in the fullness of the Spirit can be compared to a passenger who rides behind me on the motorcycle. I will say something like this, "Put your arms around me and hang on. Do what I do. If I lean to the left, you lean to the left; if I lean to the right, you lean to the right." The song, "Leaning on the Everlasting Arms" gets at it.

The question is not, "Do I have all the Spirit?" But "Does the Spirit have all of me?"

Spirit-filled Friendships

A Spirit-filled person will live the way Jesus lived, which included many different dynamics. Jesus was a relational person—a friend to all kinds. He kicked around with social dropouts and ate with them (Matthew 9:11; John 15:1). He modeled being a friend to sinners (Matthew 11:19). The paralytic sinner must have been surprised to hear Jesus' first word to him, "Friend." The apostles were in the upper room on the night they abandoned Jesus. He knew they would soon not admit they knew him, yet he said to them, "Greater love has no one than this, that he lay down his life for his friends. You are my friends if you do what I command. I no longer call you servants . . . Instead, I have called you friends. . ." (John 15:13-15). Judas led the mob to arrest Him, but Jesus greeted Judas with, "Friend" (Matthew 26:50). Looking back on those kinds of scenes, the apostles may have meditated many times about their experiences. It is not

Needed: Spirit-Filled Leaders

easy to be a friend to someone who engages in a negatively different lifestyle. But the Father, Son, and Holy Spirit do that with us.

I was the top sergeant over fifty air traffic controllers at a mobile squadron in Japan when 6'4" Sergeant Max arrived to be the commanding officer's right hand man. Sgt. Max had not been there long before coming to the office drunk. Two or three months later he did it again and this time urinated in his uniform; however, no disciplinary action was taken. Three of us other sergeants went to the Colonel to discuss the effects such conduct and lack of discipline were having on the younger troops.

Then the Colonel told us about Sgt. Max who was in Intelligence with top-secret information about battle plans and the movement of troops during World War II. The Germans captured him, brought him to a concentration camp, and tortured him to get secret information, but Max refused to cooperate. The Germans captured Max's brother, brought him to the same camp, had the two kneel side-by-side, put a German Luger (pistol) to the brother's head, and said, "Sergeant, you tell us what we want or we will blow the brains out of your brother." Max refused. The guards pulled the trigger, and blood and bones from his brother's head splattered all over Max's face. Eventually the desired information became outdated, but the Germans continued to torture Max until the end of the war. When the allies came into the camp, 6'4" Max weighed less than 70 pounds. He was flown to Walter Reed Hospital outside Washington D.C. where he was hospitalized for nearly four years.

Near the time to dismiss him, the medical team reported that Sgt. Max could become a candidate for skid row because of all the drugs and painkillers given to him over the years; however, he wanted to remain in the military, and the medical team recommended it. But if so, his medical records should reveal that he might occasionally come to work after drinking too much, but no disciplinary action should be taken because of what he did for his country.

Isn't it true that it is easier to be friends with someone when we understand the root of that person's life? I went to Sgt. Max and became his friend, and asked him to call me every time he felt like he might drink too much. Sometimes I would get a call at 1:00 AM, and would stay with him until we both reported for duty. To be a friend does not mean we have to approve or like that other person's actions, but it does mean we need to develop an affectionate caring relationship.

Are members of your church known as "friends of sinners"—of people who do not attend church and those who do, but who have diverse kinds of not-so-nice lifestyles? If not, are we really functioning as Christ's disciples, ambassadors, and representatives of God, who are under the influence of the fruit of the Spirit? Or is it that we do not want to be known like that?

Spirit-filled Pleasures

Jesus revealed one of the secrets of His life when he said, "The one who sent me is with me; he has not left me alone, for **I always do what pleases him**" (John 8:29. Bold print mine). Why would anyone do everything to please someone else? Love is the reason. Jesus was in love with the Father, and only if we are in love with Him will we be committed to please Him. We are to discover what pleases God (Ephesians 5:10); make it our goal to please Him (2 Corinthians 5:9); do everything to please Him (1 John 3:22); and live in order to please Him (1 Thessalonians 4:1). The writer of Hebrews concluded his exhortation with, "May the God of peace, who through the blood of the eternal covenant brought back from the dead our Lord Jesus, that great Shepherd of the sheep, equip you with **everything good** for doing his will, and may he work in us **what is pleasing to him** through Jesus Christ to whom be glory for ever and ever. Amen" (13:20-21. Bold print mine). A Spirit-filled person will ask questions like, "Would God like this? Would this put a smile on God's face? Would this please Him? Would Jesus do this if He were here?" and so on. For if everything the Spirit does pleases the Father, and if that same Spirit lives in us, and if we are keeping in step with the Spirit, then we will try to please God as Paul did, "We are not trying to please men but God, who tests our hearts" (1 Thessalonians 2:4). **To please the Father in the ways Jesus did is one way to measure how close we are to being conformed to the likeness of God, and thus becoming fully human in an inhuman world.**

Spirit-filled Service

Jesus prioritized service above status. He squelched the apostles caving into the culture's bent toward status when he declared that true greatness is not measured by how many servants a person has, but by how many people a person serves. On one occasion He said, "You know that the rulers of the Gentiles lord it over them, and their high officials exercise authority over them. Not so with you. Instead, whoever wants to become great among you must be your servant, and whoever wants to be first must be your slave—just as the Son of Man did not come to be served, but to serve, and give his life as a ransom for many" (Matthew 20:25-28). On the night He was betrayed, Jesus' apostles argued among themselves about which one of them was the greatest. Jesus interrupted the dispute with the following statement, "The kings of the Gentiles lord it over them; and those who exercise authority over them call themselves Benefactors. But you are not to be like that. Instead, the greatest among you should be like the youngest, and the one who rules like the one who serves. For who is greater, the one who is at the table or the one who serves? Is it not the one who is at the table? But I am among you as one who serves" (Luke 22:25-27).

Greatness is not measured by how many servants a person has, but by how many people a person serves

Jesus then modeled great servanthood by taking a towel and a basin of water to wash twenty-four dirty feet. Then He outlined the root character of a great servant when He said, "A new commandment I give you: Love one another. As I have loved you, so you must love one another. By this all men will know that you are my disciples, if you love one another" (John 13:24-35).

Spirit-filled Fruit

Jesus extended Himself to be a blessing to all kinds of people without excluding any by prejudices—God's purpose for His people (See Genesis 12:2-3; Acts 3:24-25; Galatians 3:8). People experienced the fruit of the Spirit from His words and works—love, joy, peace, patience, kindness, goodness, faithfulness, gentleness, and self-control.

Below are several relational skills that communicate the servant life of a Spirit-filled leader each of which was modeled by Jesus through His deeds and declarations; and each of which expresses various dimensions for being fully human in an inhuman world:

1. Has a balance of competence and compassion.
2. Has a balance of being flexible in methods, but inflexible in mission.
3. Being a supervisor, yet also a servant to others.
4. Does not abuse power or position.
5. Has a heart bigger than the head.
6. Has the tongue under control.
7. Is open to suggestions.
8. Is available and approachable.
9. Is not a respecter of a person's gender, race, or economical position.
10. Gives credit to others.
11. Considers the importance of every member of the team.
12. Matches peoples' aptitudes to their responsibilities.
13. Gives authority for people to carry out their responsibilities.
14. Trusts people with their responsibilities.
15. Encourages.
16. Unifies.
17. Knows how to forgive and does.
18. Gives the heavenly Father credit.
19. Looks after, not just over people.
20. Applies Matthew 7:12, "So in everything do to others what you would have them do to you."
21. Sees potential in people.
22. Recognizes the MMFI need of people, "Make Me Feel Important" and does.
23. Has vision beyond the now.
24. Views people as the most valuable asset.
25. Allows soak time before making radical changes.
26. Sets high standards for self.
27. Supervises without "snoopervises".
28. Shares success with others.
29. Sees positives through the negatives.
30. Creates and maintains an environment where people enjoy working and living.

31. Discovers, taps, and releases charisma in people.
32. Doesn't turn people into workaholics.
33. Balances labor and leisure.
34. Prays for, but will not prey upon people.
35. Sets goals with practical steps for reaching them.
36. Does not take criticism personally.
37. Motivates others.
38. Looks for things people are doing right, and lets them and others know.
39. Seeks God's will in all decisions.
40. Lives to please God.
41. Is quick to listen and slow to speak.
42. Thinks before speaking.
43. Does not shoot from the lip.
44. Puts up with people it would be easy to put down.
45. Picks up, not picks on the fallen.
46. Is warm, not cold to others.
47. Doesn't keep score or try to get even.
48. Sets a schedule to read the Bible through regularly (Jesus knew Scripture well).
49. Regularly engages in diverse spiritual disciplines.
50. Does not elevate self above others.
51. Prioritizes people over property and possessions.
52. Helps others become mature.

To serve exactly as Jesus did is one way to measure how close we are to being conformed to the likeness of God

We will next consider specific disciplines that can help develop Christlikeness in order to become fully human in an inhuman world.

9

Transforming Into Christlikeness

Part One

Spirituality and Spiritual Formation

Through the ages some have tried to influence God's people to abandon His ways. But Jesus called them thieves and robbers (John 10:8). Jesus pronounced woes on one such group of "thieves" with a devastating statement, "You travel over land and sea to win a single convert, and you make the new convert twice as much a child of hell as yourself" (Matthew 23:15, NRSV). People were "harassed and helpless, like sheep without a Shepherd" (Matthew 9:36). So Jesus came to be the good shepherd dedicated to lay down His life and to invite us to follow Him. Only then could everyone have life and have it "more abundantly"—have it to the full (John 10:10, NRSV).

As the good Shepherd, Jesus came to lead us (John 10:3-4). He went ahead of us to model what it characteristically and relationally means to be fully human living in an inhuman world. He promised the gift of His own Spirit to equip us to live the way He lived. We can conform to that life only as we allow His Spirit to grow in us and flow from us, so each of us can fully develop into the kind of person we were originally created to be, and in Christ recreated to become. The transformation of our humanness back into our original created nature is what spiritual formation is about. God desires that we not only experience spiritual birth (John 3:3-12), but also that we experience spiritual maturity, "Therefore let us leave the elementary teachings. . . . and go on to maturity. . . . And God permitting, we will do so" (Hebrews 6:1-3).

As we journey toward maturity, it is important that we are on the same page with some relevant and often used terms. Here are a few of them: **Spiritual** refers to the holistic self that transcends the physical by integrating the soul (our innermost being), spirit (our mental capacity), and body (our physical activities) into a harmonious oneness. Being spiritual refers to practicing the presence of God by giving attention to the life of the Spirit as modeled by Jesus. Our spirituality is the character base from which our life flows. It is the integration (connection) of our triune self (body, soul, and spirit) with God's triune self (Father, Son, and Holy Spirit). **Spiritual formation** refers to shaping a person toward spiritual maturity. **Spiritual maturity** refers to being integrated into and dominated by God's Spirit, resulting in cooperation with God and functioning in concert with His Son, enabling that person to live beyond self for others as God's consistent representative/ambassador in all circumstances.

Aids for Maturing Us

God uses many avenues to transform us from one spiritual level to another, which include the following:

1. The liberation of the Holy Spirit (2 Corinthians 3:17-18).
2. The mercies of God (Romans 12:1-2).
3. Charisma in each Christian (Romans 12:3-8; 1 Corinthians 12:4-7; 14:12; Ephesians 4:16).
4. Human leaders (Ephesians 4:11-16).
5. Spiritual disciplines.

Spiritual maturity is to be integrated into and dominated by God's Spirit, resulting in cooperation with God and functioning in concert with His Son, enabling a person to live beyond self for others as God's consistent representative/ambassador in all circumstances

Serious Deficiency within Christianity

There is presently numerical growth in many congregations, but unfortunately not a continual collateral maturational growth among members. It is not difficult to trace part of that deficiency to colleges and seminaries that graduate leaders who are not exposed to either God's goal that Christians mature to Christlikeness or to God's ways to lead individuals and the church toward that goal. I will apply the rest of this chapter to both Christian higher education (colleges and seminaries) and to local congregations. Both are, or should be, yoked together as partners to impact the world for Christ by maturing Christians to live as Christ lived.

If members are not helping each other (Ephesians 4:16), it may be partly due to the fact they have not been equipped to do so by gifted leaders, who exist "to prepare God's people for works of service, so that the body of Christ may be built up until we all reach unity in the faith and in the knowledge of the Son of God and become mature, attaining to the whole measure of the fullness of Christ" (Ephesians 4:12-13). Leaders who do not do that prostitute their call to leadership and perpetuate churches that do not represent God well in their surrounding communities. The result can easily keep Ephesians 4:14-16 from happening, "Then we will no longer be infants, tossed back and forth by the waves, and blown here and there by every wind of teaching and by the cunning and craftiness of men in their deceitful scheming. Instead, speaking the truth in love, we will in all things grow up into him who is the Head, that is, Christ. From him the whole body, joined and held together by every supporting ligament, grows, and builds itself up in love, as each part does its work."

It is essential for Christian colleges and seminaries to develop potential leaders through a spiritual formation program that includes practical ways to actualize spiritual development toward Christlikeness, so they will be better able to lead a church toward maturity. Christian educational institutions should graduate students who have a working understanding of the nature of God, of humanity, of the culture, and of the Church, the nature and need of individual Christians, intense experiences with selected spiritual disciplines, and measurable results in their own development. This can be better accomplished through an intentional and integrated spiritual formation partnership with the curriculum, faculty-student relationships, chapel services, social activities, resident living, extracurricular activities, and planned small groups.

Leaders who do not help Christians to systematically mature toward Christlikeness prostitute their call to leadership and perpetuate churches that do not represent God well in their surrounding communities

Spirituality and Physical Well-being

Spirituality is not only essential for the spiritual health of the church, but also for the physical health of her individual members. Medical education is catching up with the realities of the Bible. While Christian higher education remains behind in exposing students to the spiritual, practical, and physical results of spiritual disciplines. Over 70% of medical schools in this country are introducing medical students to the physical benefits of spirituality. Medical schools such as Harvard University, Duke University, and George Washington University are key leaders in this cutting edge development. The Continuing Education Department of the Medical School at Harvard University offers a "Spirituality and Healing" track for physicians in the field.

Spiritual Disciplines for Maturing

Spiritual disciples are those activities and functions that shape the living Christ into our lives to the end that our thinking and living conform to and manifest the reality of the presence and character of God in all our relationships and situations. Everything God described for us to do and Jesus demonstrated is first of all for our own holistic well being, not because

God is some kind of celestial Santa Claus making a list and checking it twice to find out who is naughty and nice. Because Christians are in diverse situations and stages of development, some disciplines will be more valuable at different times than others. Several of those listed below are common; however, they are often taken for granted without giving them priority, practice, and permanence:

Fellowship

Fellowship is not optional, but is essential for spiritual formation into Christlikeness. There are two basic levels. One is the temporary connection caused by some event or happening that is external to persons, such as attending events (sports, concerts, amusement parks); working together on a project; being passengers on a plane, and so on. It is only the happening that temporarily connects people. The connection ends when the event or situation ends. That can also easily take place when people gather together to worship.

The deeper level of fellowship is formed from a common inner connection that continually binds companions who share with each other as partners. This is *koinonia* in the New Testament. It is formed when people inwardly share the same Holy Spirit making them eternal brothers and sisters. This kind of connection results from evangelism as revealed by John, "We proclaim to you what we have seen and heard, so that you also may have fellowship with us. And our fellowship is with the Father and with His Son, Jesus Christ. We write this to make our joy complete" (1 John 1:3-4). John yearned to supplement his writing with a personal touch, "I have much to write to you, but I do not want to use paper and ink. Instead, I hope to visit you and talk with you face to face, so that our joy may be complete" (2 John 1-2). God created us to partnership with others who are like-minded (Philippians 2:2).

One mark of maturity within fellowship is to not regulate and dominate others. Instead, to recognize aspects of the image of God in each other, which are packaged within the diversity of personalities, aptitudes, and charisma. And to recognize, affirm, and value individual charismas in others along with encouragement and appreciation for their use. The result will be a more healthy and happy Christian community.

It is essential that Christian colleges. seminaries, and congregations develop opportunities for Christians to engage in the *koinonia* kind of fellowship in which issues, problems, joys, sorrows, and needs are shared beyond the superficial level. Research reveals that close social relationships strengthen a person's immune systems and are more important to a person's physical health than smoking, drinking, exercise, family history, or diet (Harold Koenig, *Purpose and Power in Retirement;* Dean Ornish, *Love & Survival*).

Church Attendance and Involvement

This is not optional, but is essential for the holistic well being of Christians. Part of Jesus' development included His custom of attending the synagogue. "And Jesus grew in wisdom and stature, and in favor with God and men" (Luke 2:52). Connect that with "on the Sabbath day he went into the synagogue, as was his custom" (4:16). Each person enters Christianity as a spiritual infant with some of the same needs a physical infant has, particularly the need of others without which neither physical nor spiritual infants can properly develop. The church is the family of God, which has the responsibility to help develop His children into mature spiritual adults. The church is also referred to as the body of Christ with each member being a specific functional part. As in the physical body, so it is in the spiritual body: a cell cannot survive if disconnected from the body. Thus, Christians are not to "give up meeting together, as some are in the habit of doing" (Hebrews 10:25). The first Christians "devoted themselves to the apostles' teaching and to the fellowship, to the breaking of bread and to prayer" (Acts 2:42). God puts Christians in community with other Christians to help deliver us from the damnation of our own egos and loneliness. That deliverance enables us to more easily receive and give love. We were created to need and to love the triune God and each other. John made that clear, "Whoever loves God must also love his brother" (1 John 4:21), and "everyone who loves the Father loves his child as well" (1 John 5:1).

Human cells in Christ's body, the Church, interact with other cells to enhance nourishment for spiritual and physical health. Church attendance is a major supply depot that equips Christians for daily living. Medical science discovered "that religious involvement helps people *prevent* illness, *recover* from illness, and—most remarkably—*live longer*. The more religiously committed you are, the more likely you are to benefit" (Dale Matthews, M.D. *The Faith Factor: Proof of the Healing Power of Prayer*, 18). A classic study of 91,909 people discovered those who attended church once, twice, or more times a week did not have as many cancers, had lower blood pressure, had significantly lower death rates from coronary artery disease, emphysema, and from other diseases (Ibid., 19-23).

Christian colleges and seminaries should require regular church involvement as part of graduation requirements. To not do so is equal to a medical school granting an M.D. degree without requiring an internship.

Service

Service/ministry is not an option, but is essential for Christians to mature spiritually. All Christians have charisma to use for the good of others in order to meet needs, encourage, strengthen, comfort, and help build up the body of Christ on earth (Ephesians 4:7-16; 1 Corinthians 12:4-30; 14:3-12; Romans 12:4-8; 1 Peter 4:10-11).

Medical science discovered that people who volunteer service have a more positive outlook on life; an increased rate of nitric oxide, which improves the immune system, heart, and blood pressure; and after factoring all other related issues, are less likely to die than those that do not volunteer (Koenig, *Purpose and Power in Retirement*, 84-90).

The specific kinds of ministries depend upon several factors, such as the immediate needs and opportunities, as well as the server's personality, abilities, and charisma. The kinds of services are endless, which include such specifics as listening, writing, preaching, teaching, bearing with another's burdens, forgiving, praying, giving time and money, being present, holding the tongue, modeling, leading, physically helping, accepting help from another, contacting and networking with others to help, going beyond what is expected, visiting, extending friendship, inviting, using hobbies to benefit others, singing, playing a musical instrument, sharing in small groups, being transparent, initiating acts of mercy, volunteering in areas that match abilities to another's needs, being responsible with work expectations and assignments, and so on. The body of Christ—the church—matures as each part (member) does its work (Ephesians 4:16).

Christian education should require a certain amount of volunteer work/service from students to better equip them in practical ways to lead congregations into discovering the charisma of members, the needs of members, the needs of people in the surrounding area, and how to connect those needs with specific ways gifted members can serve them through the church and through non-church related activities.

Prayer

Prayer is not optional, but is essential for spiritual and physical health of individual Christians and for the maturity of a congregation. In recent years scientific research has discovered many benefits to prayer that have captured the attention of the medical field. In 1995 the *Journal of the American Medical Association* published an article, "Should Physicians Prescribe Prayer for Health?" The article reported evidence of the benefits of prayer for physical health. A previous non-believer, Larry Dossey, M.D., studied many double blind studies about the effects of prayer, became a believer, and wrote a *New York Times* best-selling book, *Prayer Is Good Medicine.* Dossey's research motivated him to question himself, "Should I be using prayer on behalf of my patients?" And his answer was, "I decided that *not* doing so was the equivalent of withholding a needed medication or surgical procedure, and I began to pray for my patients daily." He then raised a potential issue, "Will we reach a point where physicians who ignore prayer will be judged guilty of malpractice" (65-66)?

Early Christians devoted themselves to prayer (Acts 2:42). Paul included something about prayer in most of his writings. Over recent decades, the mid-week prayer service in most churches has been canceled, and there is little time allotted for members to pray during worship services. Christian higher education can help reverse that trend by not only modeling meaningful and diverse prayers in residence hall meetings, classrooms, and chapel, but also by developing a Spiritual Development Program to introduce students to and engage them in various kinds of prayers, such as prayers of confession, breath prayers (short verbal notes to God), relinquishing prayers (giving each specific activity to God), prayers questioning God, praise prayers, prayers of complaints, intercessory prayers (going to bat for others), thanksgiving prayers, requesting prayers, prayers for miracles, forgiving prayers (letting go of grudges and desires for revenge), celebrating prayers, and many more, all of which appear in the Psalms.

Anyone can spend at least an hour a day in prayer by planning time for prayer, and by using dead times—those time when chats with God can be done while doing other things such as driving, waiting, getting ready to go somewhere, exercising, working, muting out television commercials, walking from one place to another, and so on. Jesus once asked His apostles why they could not pray one hour, and they did not know how to answer Him (Mark 14:37-40). Would we?

Isn't it interesting that very few Christian colleges, seminaries, and churches offer even one course on prayer? Such a course should include the biblical theology of prayer, different kinds of prayers, reading prayers of others, making a journal of prayers, and so on. To neglect teaching this, as well as other disciplines, is equal to not teaching surgical students the various tools necessary for successful surgeries. See Appendix 2 where nine different kinds of prayer are described with steps for praying them.

Bible Reading

It is one thing to read the Bible in order to have good reports on papers in college, or get kudos in a reading program in a church, but it is another thing to read it in order to discover and develop good relationships with God, self, and others. It is one thing to correctly analyze the text, but it is another thing to allow the text to analyze us and then to correctly apply it.

It is important to read the Bible through at least once a year. Here is one possible approach for doing that:

1. Count the number of pages in the New Testament; divide that number by 365, and read that many pages each day. The person will read through the New Testament once a year.
2. Read one chapter in Proverbs every day that corresponds with the calendar date. The person will read through Proverbs once a month.

3. Read one Psalm a day. The person will read through Psalms 2 1/3 times a year.
4. Subtract the number of pages read in Psalms and Proverbs from the sum total number of pages in the Old Testament, divide that number by 365, and read that many pages each day, The person will annually read through the Old Testament once a year.
5. Obtain the Bible on CD's or cassettes. Then listen to it while driving, walking, working, and so on.

In many Bibles, a person will need to read only 3-5 pages a day to annually read it through, depending upon the size if the print and footnotes, which will not lengthen the reading time. A person reading through the Bible that often will see concepts and interconnections not gleaned from any other source. Such a reader should use different versions, translations, and paraphrases in order to get a better grasp of the content.

It is also important for students to experience *Meditatio Scripturarum* or *Lectio Divina*, which has been practiced for centuries, particularly in monasteries. This kind of reading internalizes and personalizes the texts by inserting self into the situations or concepts of the text. Richard Foster describes it this way, "The written Word becomes a living word addressed to you." When Dietrich Bonhoeffer started the Finkenwalde Seminary, he required everyone to daily spend one-half hour meditating on a text, and recommended they spend an entire week on the same text. Soren Kierkeegard called this approach the "contemporaneity" of Scripture. Alexander Whyte believed when the text is read this way it becomes an autobiography of the reader.

This approach requires the person to imagine personally being inside the situation being reported so the reader hears the thunder; sees the lightning strike; feels the touch of Jesus' hand; hears the shouts of people in the street; sees the shape of trees, and color of the leaves; smells the fish; hears the waves of the sea kissing the beach; tastes the salt in the water of Dead Sea; touches the hem of Jesus' robe; senses the excitement as the dead daughter opens her eyes; sits with 49 other people who sit together and receive the little lad's fish and bread. Doing this requires the reader to read the text out loud several times; the first time to picture the situation; the second time to see and feel the situation; the following times to insert self into the text in order to let it move from the reader's eyes to the mind, the feelings, and the applications. Reading the story of the Good Samaritan several times is one example (Luke 10:30-35). With each reading, insert yourself into the life and internalize the feelings of a different character in the story:

1. As the robber, ask, "How and when have I been like a robber?"
2. As the one beaten, ask, "How and when have I been wounded by others, and how did it feel to be abandoned?"
3. As the priest or the Levite, ask, "How and when have I been like one of them?"
4. As the Samaritan, ask, "How and when have I been like that?"
5. As the beast of burden, ask, "How and when have I been used like that?"
6. As the Innkeeper, ask, "How and when have I been like that?"

Write a journal that includes the above with new commitments related to the parable. Be specific and transparent with the applications. This kind of reading takes us from being an observer on the outside to being a participant on the inside.

Silence and Solitude

Dietrich Bonhoeffer wrote, "Let him who cannot be alone beware of community. Let him who is not in community beware of being alone." We need to be alone to help realize the value of self, to sense the presence and love of God, to acknowledge our vulnerabilities, and to recommit ourselves to contribute to the community as a refreshed person buoyed up by God's encounter with us.

We live in a culture of noise and activities, and often enter a worship service to more noise and activities. Jesus began His ministry by getting alone with God for forty days, and later often withdrew from activities and noise. We need to spend alone times with God in order to reduce our addictions to productivity, to being hurried, to being workaholics, "activityholics", "busyaholics", "goaholics", and "haveaholics". If the devil cannot make us too bad, he can easily make us too busy to think we cannot slow down to relish the presence of God.

It is possible that some use busyness, television, noise, entertainment, and so on, to eat away time as a rationale for disengaging from thinking and from relating to others. Instead of healthy relaxation, it is possible that such time consuming activities numb the brain and keep a person from looking inward to self and outward to others.

One benefit of solitude is silence. Several texts emphasize quietness. "Be still before the Lord and wait patiently for him" (Psalm 37:7). "Be still and know [experience] that I am the God" (Psalm 46:10, brackets mine). "He leads me beside quiet waters" (Psalm 23:2). God whispers as well as shouts. God knows how to back off, "For a long time I have kept silent, I have been quiet and held myself back" (Isaiah 42:14). The Lord came to Elijah not in the noise of the wind, the shattering of the rocks, nor the roaring of the fire, but in a gentle whisper that changed him (1 Kings 19:11-13). There were times Jesus said, "Be still", and both external and internal storms vanished. Silence provides the kind of environment during which one can reflect and not react, engage and not just exist, and be intentional and not just passive.

Medical science reports that living in the midst of noise and crowds without relief weakens the immune system, increases blood pressure, elevates the heart rate, and increases the level of stress.

In the midst of a goaholic, workaholic, rushaholic, and busyaholic world, it is prudent to develop quiet times. Here are some steps:

1. Take advantage of little quiet times during the day, such as right after getting up, during waiting times, muting out commercials on television, and turning off the television and radio.
2. Select a private place and a set time each day to visit that place alone.
3. Practice being quick to hear and slow to speak.
4. Practice spending one entire day without saying a word.
5. Plan a quiet retreat at least once a year for meditation and prayer.

Meditation

The Psalmist wrote that one thing he desired was to meditate in God's temple (27:4). The Christian's physical body is identified in the New

Testament as God's temple (1 Corinthians 6:19; Ephesians 2:22; 1 Peter 2:5; Hebrews 2:9). God's ancient people mediated upon God's Word (Psalm 1:2), His precepts (Psalm 119:15), His declarations (Psalm 119:47), His promises (Psalm 119:148), His majesty and wonderful works (Psalm 145:5). Paul listed several positive subjects upon which to meditate, so the peace of God that surpasses understanding would be with us (Philippians 4:4-9). Here is a meditative practice:

1. Sit in a chair with feet on the floor and hands on the lap with palms up.
2. Close the eyes.
3. Relax the muscles from top to bottom.
4. Breath in and out slowly.
5. Visualize a peaceful scene, such as a garden, a calm ocean, a peaceful valley, or sitting at Jesus' feet.
6. Select a characteristic of God, or one activity He has done for others or self, or one scene in Jesus' life.
7. Reflect for 10 minutes upon what you selected in #6. Keep focusing upon it and imagine you are crawling inside the scene and are a part of the situation.
8. Then sing or whisper words to a song.

Today, there is little time in most worship services in this country for people to meditate in silence. Some refer to periods of silence as "dead times" that spoil the mood. It would be helpful for colleges or seminaries to plan times for meditation in chapel services, resident devotions, small group meetings, and classroom experiences; and for congregations to plan a meditation time in worship services; and for family units to plan meditation times when all members are together; and for individuals to plan meditation times. To fail to plan for meditation times is to plan to fail in meditation. See Appendix 2.

In the next chapter we will explore other essential disciplines.

10

Transforming Into Christlikeness

Part Two

One reason some may be negative about the relevance of the Church could be partly related to the fact that members have failed to take transformation into Christlikeness (godliness) seriously. Is it possible that we may be giving the surrounding culture more influence in shaping our moral conscience than the spiritual Church? The media outside us may have more formational influence than the Master inside us.

Because God desires that we do not remain spiritual infants, He shared many different disciplines that can help us become more fully human in an inhuman world in spite of all the cultural attractions that can easily delight us, distract us, and distance us from God in whose image and likeness we were created (Genesis 1:26), and from Christ in whom we were recreated (2 Corinthians 5:17),

Our surrounding culture may have more influence shaping our moral conscience than the church. The media outside of us may have more influence that the Master inside of us

Tongue Control

Tongue control is not optional, but is essential for becoming fully human in an inhuman world. I am not aware of any book that lists tongue control as an essential spiritual discipline. However, the Bible has more to say about the use of the tongue than any other part of the physical body. James directly connected controlling the tongue to spiritual maturity, "We all stumble in many ways. If anyone is never at fault in what he says, he is a perfect man, able to keep his whole body in check" (James 3:2). The word "perfect" translates the Greek word *teleios*, which means "mature." The tongue affects and reflects the whole person. If used wrongly it "corrupts the whole person, sets the whole course of his life on fire, and is itself set on fire by hell" (3:6). Jesus revealed it, "For the things that come out of the mouth come from the heart, and these make a man unclean" (Matthew 15:18). While no human law can control the tongue, God's Spirit can because His Spirit is the "pilot" who can control the rudder on our "tongue-ship" (James 3:7-8). James summed up the holistic effect of the tongue when he shared, "If any think they are religious, and do not bridle their tongues but deceive their hearts, their religion is worthless" (James 1:26). He then immediately linked control of the tongue to compassion for people, "Religion that is pure and undefiled before God, the Father, is this: to care for orphans and widows in their distress, and to keep oneself unstained by the world" (verse 27, NRSV).

We grieve the Holy Spirit when we use the tongue to hurt others (Ephesians 4:29-30). Consequently, spiritual development should include biblical research and personal assessment on the use of the tongue. Research could begin by reading through Proverbs and record every reference to the tongue. Then keep a week-long or month-long record of the times your own tongue helped or hurt others. That should include times your verbal or "inner tongue" puts self down in negative self-talk. Here are some positive uses of the tongue:

1. Help, don't hurt people.
2. Build up, don't tear down others.
3. Count down, don't blast off.
4. Don't shoot from the lip.

5. Think before speaking, for there may be nothing contributive to say.
6. Give strokes, not pokes.
7. Repeated crosswords are acceptable in puzzles, but not in people.
8. About people who hurt you, don't rub it in, but rub it out.
9. Pick up, don't pick on the fallen ones.
10. Be warm, not cold.
11. Be positive, not negative.
12. Say to and about others what you would want them to say to and about you.
13. Say to and about others what Jesus would say.
14. Never participate in gossip, whether it is true or not.
15. Never slander another.
16. Be gentle, not grouchy.
17. "He who loves a quarrel loves sin" (Proverbs 17:19; see also 2 Timothy 2:24-26).

The attitudes used when speaking will eventually return to the speaker. Don't believe that little saying, "Sticks and stones may break my bones, but words will never hurt me." Words can hurt as well as help.

While no human law can control the tongue, God's Spirit can because His Spirit is the "pilot" who can control the rudder on our "tongue-ship

Terrible things happen within congregations and personal relationships when this powerful instrument is used wrongly.

Forgiveness

Forgiveness is essential, but not easy. C.S. Lewis wrote that forgiveness is a lovely idea until there is someone to forgive. Ben Franklin once wrote that doing an injury puts you below your enemy; revenging one makes you only even with him; but forgiving sets you above him.

There is not enough education about forgiveness in either Christian higher education or churches. However, secular institutions have not been as silent as Christian institutions. In recent years major newspapers and magazines have included lead articles about forgiveness. These include *The Chicago Tribune, The Chronicle of Higher Education, The Journal of Personality and Social Psychology, The Yale Journal for Humanities in Medicine, Health Magazine, The Christian Science Monitor, Reader's Digest*, and *Christianity Today.*

Major universities are doing research on the benefits of forgiveness. For instance, Stanford University developed the on going "Stanford Forgiveness Project" that studies the effects of forgiveness. The continuing education department of the Medical School at Harvard University offers a course, "The Importance of Forgiveness" in its Spirituality and Healing track. Some of the leading researchers in the field of forgiveness include Robert Enright (University of Wisconsin), Frederic Luskin (Stanford University), Christina Puchaiski (George Washington University), the late Lewis Smedes (Fuller Theological Seminary), Carl Thoresen (Stanford University), and Everett Worthington (Virginia Commonwealth University). It is time Christian colleges, seminaries, and congregations began to catch up with secular institutions to study, teach, and apply what forgiveness is and is not, the positive benefits of forgiveness, and the negative results of holding grudges.

There is not enough education about forgiveness in either Christian higher education or churches

On several occasions Jesus emphasized the essentiality of forgiveness, "For if you forgive men when they sin against you, your heavenly Father will also forgive you. But if you do not forgive men their sins, your Father will not forgive your sins" (Matthew 6:14-15). That was Jesus' only comment about the Lord's Prayer, which He reinforced elsewhere, "And when you stand praying, if you hold anything against anyone forgive him, so that your Father in heaven may forgive your sins" (Mark 11:25). Jesus made it clear that the Father will not keep forgiving debt collectors—those who keep and nurture grudges, but He will for debt "cancellers"—those who practice canceling debts of others (Matthew 18:23-35). There is no limit to the number of times to forgive the same person (Matthew 18:21-22). We are expected to forgive each other, "just as in Christ God forgave you" (Ephesians 4:32). Paul linked the preceding statement about forgiveness to being imitators of God as people who live a life of love and sacrifice (Ephesians 5:1-2; see also Colossians 3:12-13). It takes agape-style love to let go of a grudge or bitterness we think we deserve to keep. In the Colossian passage, forgiveness is linked to kindness, compassion, humility, gentleness, patience, putting up with people, unity, peace, love, and thankfulness—all of which are essential for forgiving others. Claiming to be a mature Christian while not forgiving is a spiritual oxymoron.

To Forgive as God does is one way to measure how close we are to being conformed to the likeness of God

The Church must stop being the only army that shoots its own wounded or abandons them on the spiritual battlefields of life. We need to assess whether we are "debt collectors" or "debt cancellers." Perhaps we could start an assessment by keeping a record of the times we were hurt and our responses when forgiven.

What forgiveness is not:

(1) Not the same as forgetfulness, nor does it call for a person to forget. A woman will not forget being raped. Family members will not forget someone murdering another family member or a drunken driver crashing into a car and killing a loved one. Only God is able to forget all sins He forgives (Isaiah 43:25; Jeremiah 31:34; Hebrews 8:12; 10:17).
(2) Not condoning or dismissing the offense as if it did not hurt or was insignificant.
(3) Not pardoning a crime committed against you. That is a legal matter to be decided by the courts.
(4) Not reconciliation, but it is willing to reconcile when possible. It takes both the offended and the offender to reconcile; however, the offender may not wish to be reconciled or be available for it.

Claiming to love God while not forgiving contradicts reality

What forgiveness involves:

(1) It is a choice; it does not come automatically.
(2) It is releasing any desire that the offender be hurt or paid back in some way.
(3) It accepts the consequences of having been hurt without designing the slightest revenge (Romans 12:17-19).
(4) It wishes some good for the other person (Romans 12:21).
(5) It prays for, not preys upon, the other person (Matthew 5:44).
(6) It does good for that other person, if able with an opportunity to do so (see Matthew 5:43-48. Note the word "perfect" in verse 48 means "mature").

Some stages leading toward forgiveness:

(1) Realize it is a choice that only the offended person can make.
(2) Realize it requires a disposition that comes from attitudes of the heart.
(3) Quit repeating to yourself or to others what that other person did.
(4) Draw from the fruit of the Spirit, such as love, patience, kindness, gentleness, and self control.
(5) Put yourself in the other person's place, and do what you would want done were you in that person's situation.
(6) Release the offense and the offender to God who is at work in you to forgive through you.
(7) Tell the person whom you have forgiven what it means to you to forgive and to have been forgiven.

Medical researcher Everett Worthington teaches the REACH approach for forgiving: R—Recall the hurt. That is, identify it and admit it; E—Empathize with the one who hurt you. That is, put yourself in that person's situation; A—Altruistic gift of forgiveness. That is, reflect on the times you have hurt others and recall feeling the weight taken off you when you were forgiven. That helps free you to give the same gift to another; C—

Commit to forgive. That is, do something about it, such as to make a certificate of forgiveness, write a letter to the offender, even though you may not send it; make a phone call to the offender, even though that may be painful, wish forgiveness in your heart. H—Hold on to forgiveness during times of doubting. That is, to not allow a momentary bad feeling about the offender cause you to think you have not forgiven. In summation: (1) **Let it go**—stop rehearsing it and wishing some injury to that person. (2) **Let it glow**—wish well for that person, and if possible do something good for that person. (3) **Let it grow**—practice forgiveness with every hurt to develop a propensity, a perspective, and a power for forgiving in order to become a consistently forgiving person. Keep practicing forgiveness, because "He who covers an offense promotes love" (Proverbs 17:9;10:12). Love is the mark of being a Christian (John 13:34-35) and the relational way others can know what God is like (1 John 4:12).

To Forgive as God does is one way to measure how close we are to the likeness of God, and thus becoming fully human in an inhuman world

Facing temptations

Although all are tempted, it is possible that some congregational leaders and members are not helped to face temptations with teachings about the value of being tempted, the security of being tempted, and practical ways to resist yielding.

The value of being tempted is that God gave us freedom to choose. Every time we do not yield, we communicate to God that we love Him and are pleasing Him—not because we have to, but because we want to.

The security of being tempted is found in God's promise that He will never allow us to be tempted above what we are able to endure, and that we will never be tempted with things that are not common to others who have conquered them (1 Corinthians 10:13). The security of being tempted is also found in the fact that Jesus was tempted in every way we are, but without sin. And because of that, we can go to Him when we are tempted and find grace to help us during our times of weakness and need (Hebrews 4:15-16).

James outlined how we are tempted, "But one is tempted by one's own desire, being lured and enticed by it" (James 1:14, NRSV). Most desires are God-given, such as desires for hunger, thirst, sex, love, acceptance, pleasure, security, and so on. As long as we keep those desires within God's guardrails, we have a broad option of choices we can make without sinning. God provided a wonderful world in which those desires can be met, such as food for hunger, liquid for drink, and the opposite gender for sex. God's commandments about moral issues function like guardrails along a dangerous mountain roads. However, the devil knows all about our desires, God's world, and His guardrails. So the devil lures, a word used for fishing. The fish sees the lure, but not the hidden hook. But the lure **looked** so authentic and fulfilling. The devil also entices. That was a word used in hunting, such as the fake duck call that signals the lake is a safe haven for ducks. But the "call" **sounded** so real. The devil lures us with what looks so fulfilling and entices us with what sounds so real by going just beyond the guardrails, such as gluttony for food, drunkardness for drink, and adultery for sex. When we chase the lures and enticements beyond the guardrails (outside the box), we allow the devil to fertilize the egg of our desires. Then a conception takes place, and we give birth to sin (James 1:15). That is what it means to fall short of the glory [character] of God (Romans 3:23, brackets mine).

The devil lures us with what looks so fulfilling and entices us with what sounds so real by going just beyond the guardrails

How do we respond to the attractiveness of "outside-the-box" lures and enticements when they are connected to our God-given desires and to elements in the God-given world for meeting those desires? We can get accustomed to and practice the handles of "No, Go, Whoa, and Glow".

(1) Say, "NO" to the person through whom the temptation comes. Say what you would say if someone were about to break into your car, "No! Stop that right now." The devil does not like courage, and will flee from those who firmly resist (James 4:7). Weak cowards will not be in heaven (Revelation 21:8).

(2) Say, "GO" to the environment. "I'm out of here." Certain environments are hot with temptations. Do what you would do if

you heard the words, "Fire! This place is on fire!" I doubt you would respond with, "I want to stick around and get warmer."

(3) Say, "WHOA" to fantasizing thoughts. Inwardly yell, "Whoa" as if speaking to a runaway horse; hit the brakes or turn off the ignition as if driving a runaway car headed toward a cliff. Paul wrote, ". . . make no provision for the flesh, to gratify its desires" (Romans 13:14, NRSV). The NIV put it this way, ". . . do not think about how to gratify the desires of the sinful nature."

(4) "GLOW" with the full armor of God when on the battlefield with the devil firing away. Stand strong with truth, righteousness [proper relationships], peace with God and others, faith, salvation, the Holy Spirit, prayer, and the companionship of fellow Christians who help each other stay alert and be victorious (Ephesians 6:10-18. Brackets are mine).

Make a commitment to declare, "Buzz off, Satan. I am not a wet fish for your lure with its hidden hook or a bird-brained fowl for your fake call. I am a person created and recreated in the image and likeness of God. I am a child of the heavenly Father. I live here temporarily, but my permanent citizenship is heaven. I am God's to please, not yours to pervert. So buzz off and go back to hell where you belong. I am determined to become fully human in an inhuman world. The heavenly Father promised I can grow up to be like Jesus. Since that is my project, goodbye to you, Satan."

Small groups in the church or college could function as accountability groups in which time members share temptations they face since the last meeting and their responses to those temptations. This is a time for members to give each other encouragement instead of excluding them, and support instead of severing them. Each member should sign a commitment statement of honesty and mutual trust with promise to never repeat outside the group whatever was shared in the group.

Generosity

Why do some preachers preach so much about things mentioned so few times in the Bible, while preaching so little about some things mentioned so many times in the Bible, such as generosity with time and treasures? On the one hand, doing or not doing so may reflect what was prioritized or not prioritized during congregational teaching and preaching and during ministerial education. On the other hand, it may primarily reflect the pressure of living in a culture addicted to having and not to giving. Having and maintaining a proper balance of getting and giving is not easy for some. It takes godly courage to clearly face and to boldly challenge modern ideologies and idolatries. Idolatry refers to establishing an allegiance to something other than God for either personal or national security while giving lip service to God. Much of our Western culture is addicted to commercialism and "accumulationalism" against which God takes a hard stand.

People hold to at least one of four different attitudes about money and possessions: (1) what is mine is mine, and what I do not use for myself I will save for myself. (2) What is mine is mine, and I will spend it all for myself. (3) What is yours is also mine, and I will take it when I want it. (4) What is mine is God's, and it is His to use to advance His purpose on earth. Isn't it true that most of us could live more simply so others can simply live?

Research reveals that richer people share proportionally less than those not rich. A 1997-98 survey discovered those with incomes under $10,000 gave 4.3% of their incomes to charity, but much richer college graduates between the ages of 24-34 gave only 1.6%. The excuse some preachers give for their congregations being poor givers proportionally is that their members have lower incomes than other congregations. However, the poorest person in Jesus' ministry was a model for the rich (Mark 12:41-44). And the poorest congregations in Paul's ministry were models for richer congregations (2 Corinthians 8:1-6). So the answer is not in the members' resources, but in their resolves.

It is important for Christian higher educational institutions to graduate students who are not only committed to the ideas of generosity, but also practice it before entering leadership roles in the church. There is enough in the Bible for a semester course on this topic. It was first recorded in the giving of Cain and Abel (Genesis 4:3-5). Abel gave out of faith (Hebrews 11:4) the best he had—the firstlings of his flock, thus not knowing more would follow. However, Cain evidently short-changed God by having brought "an offering" without any premium description of it, and without

Transforming Into Christlikeness, Part Two

it being described as an offering of faith in Hebrews 11:4. But God disregarded Cain's gift. They both knew what God expected, because faith comes from hearing the word of God (Romans 10:17). Is it possible that people do not give proportionally well because they have not clearly heard God's word about this essential discipline? That word includes the following:

(1) The first mention of the tithe was Abram giving Melchizedek a tithe (Genesis 14:17-20). From that time, a tithe remained a cardinal practice of Judaism.

(2) In the Old Testament the tithe was gathered every third year to give to those who could not help themselves (Deuteronomy 14:28-29). I wonder how God would bless a congregation that committed herself to give the collected tithes to the poor every third year? Isn't it interesting that the text in the New Testament leaders often quote for giving money on Sunday was Paul's instruction to put money aside not for a building program or for salaries, but for the poor in another country (1 Corinthians 16:1-4)? The most popular text used today to motivate people to give generously was about giving money to the poor (2 Corinthians chapters 8, 9).

(3) God commanded farmers in the Old Testament not to harvest the sides of their fields so the poor could gather the leftovers for their food (Leviticus 19:9-10).

(4) God linked His people to Sodom and Gomorrah when they kept up religious rituals, but did not relieve the oppressed, nor take care of orphans and widows (Isaiah 1:10-17).

(5) God records those who help the poor as having given Him a loan (Proverbs 19:17).

(6) We defile God and show Him contempt when we bring Him only leftovers and inferior possessions (Malachi 1: 6-9).

(7) We rob God by not giving tithes and offerings. God will bless us if we do not shortchange Him, and pagan nations will take note of our relationship with God. That is one effective way to witness (Malachi 3:6-12).

(10) He who oppresses the poor shows contempt for their Maker, but whoever is kind to the needy honors God (Proverbs 14:31).

It is possible that robbing God, mentioned in the last book of the Old Testament, was not related as much to stealing as it was to not helping needy people from the wages of our work. Paul addressed this in the New Testament, "He who has been stealing must steal no longer, but must work, doing something useful with his own hands, **that he may have something to share with those in need**" (Ephesians 4:28.Ephasis mine).

Although the tithe is not commanded for Christians in the New Testament, there is little reason to **not believe** early Christians gave it and more. Why? Because for the first ten years of Christianity all members were Jews or converts to Judaism who were already committed to giving the tithe. They would surely not have given less nor needed prodding to give the tithe. Their modeling of tithing would no doubt have motivated Gentile Christians who joined them later.

Those early Christians were transformed from legalistic giving to "lovalistic" giving, because they were impacted by the inner presence and power of the Holy Spirit and by the grace and generosity of Jesus who unselfishly gave Himself for others. Jesus challenged any reluctance for sharing generously by his many teachings about it. A sampling includes Luke 12:13-21; 16:10-15; 16:19-31; Matthew 6:19-24; 25: 34-46. One way to lay up for ourselves treasures in heaven is by using our money and possessions in ways that will help others become Christians, get to heaven, and welcome us when we get there (Luke 16:9).

The first Christians practiced the discipline of generosity (Acts 2:44-45). God loves generosity when done with the right attitude (2 Corinthians 9:7). Probably, as He did with Cain, He continues not to have a high regard of those who give with wrong attitudes and reasons (See Matthew 6:3-4; 23:23-24; Acts 5:3-11). The practical theology of generous giving developed in 2 Corinthians chapters 8 and 9 is significant.

To be generous as God is generous is one way to measure how close we are to being conformed to the likeness of God

Medical science discovered that people who are generous become released from the addiction to having and wanting more, which reduces stress, helps prevent health problems, and contributes to a longer life (Harold Koenig, *Purpose and Power in Retirement,* 42, 148). The Christian psychiatrist Koenig also wrote, "A person will never be economically secure enough until he or she actually begins to practice generosity. Somehow being generous reduces one's anxiety about financial security. Being generous makes people feel richer, wealthier, and less in need of more wealth" (113). He also noted, "the generous person likes himself more and others like him a lot better as well" (114). The French politician and author Alexis de Tocqueville noted the opposite after visiting this country. He wrote, "I have seen the freest and best-educated of men in circumstances the happiest to be found in the world. It seemed to me that a cloud habitually hung on their brow and they seemed serious and almost sad in their pleasures. They never stopped thinking of the good things they have not got. They clutch everything."

Engaging spiritual disciplines for spiritual formation into Christlikeness has benefits not only for individuals, but also for families, and for local and global communities.

For families

Churches which introduce spiritual formation into the life of their families will make a difference in family issues. Through these families the immediate culture can be significantly improved as revealed by many different studies about the effects of spiritual development in families, such as the following:

- Reduces suicide rate, drug abuse, truancy, and sexual activities of children. Cubbin and Cubbin, Thompson, Hans, and Allen in "Families Under Stress: What Makes Them Resilient." *Journal and Consumer Sciences,* 89 (3), 2-12, 1997.
- Lowers instances of adolescent deviant behavior. Litchfield, Thomas, and Bid in "Dimensions of Religiosity as Mediators in Relations Between Parenting and Adolescent Deviant Behavior." *Journal of Adolescent Research* 12 (2), 199-226, 1997.
- Advances prosocial values, behaviors, and negatively related delinquency of substance abuse, premature sexual involvement, and suicidal ideation and attempts. Tharle, Vance, Najman, Embelton, and Foster in "Church Attendance, Religious

Affiliation, and Parental Responses to Sudden Infant Death, Neonatal Death, and Still Birth." *Omega* 31 (1), 51-58, 1995.
- Lowers levels of materialism among youth. Lee, Rice, Gillespie in "Family Worship Patterns and their Correlation with Adolescent Behavior and Belief." *Journal for the Scientific Study of Religion* 36 (3), 272-381, 1997.
- Reduces physical diseases and thus decreases medical bills of the members. We will explore this in chapter 12.

For the local and global communities

What happens in the life of parents affects the children. What happens in the life of children affects the school. What happens in the life of the school affects the immediate community. What happens in the life of the community affects the county. What happens in the life of the county affects the state. What happens in the life of the state affects the nation. What happens in the life of the nation affects the world.

But how will we look and live as we mature into Christlikeness that helps transform congregations, families, and the surrounding culture?

We will peek into that in the next chapter.

11

How Then Shall We Live?

The Vine and the Branches

On the night Jesus was arrested He spent several hours in the upper room teaching His apostles about their relationships with Him, the Holy Spirit, the heavenly Father, and one another. It would be prudent for Christians to give more attention to the upper room events. After all, the apostle John devoted one quarter of his Gospel to what was said and done in the room that night. The kinds of things did and said throughout His ministry are summarized in the upper room with the focus being on the intimate relationship Jesus would have with His people following His death, resurrection, and ascension.

It is possible that John intended everything in his Gospel to reflect and demonstrate Jesus' statement, "I am the true vine" (John 15:1). "True" refers to something that squares with reality. If Jesus is the true vine, there must have been a false one around. From antiquity, a false vine was any pagan religion. God planted Judaism as His vine to produce good fruit, but eventually the Israelites produced bad fruit instead (Isaiah 5:1-7). Because of their continual bad fruit, Judaism eventually became another false vine. God asked, "Now you dwellers in Jerusalem and men of Judah, judge between me and my vineyard. What more could have been done for my vineyard, than I have done for it? When I looked for good grapes, why did it yield only bad?" (5:3-4). The house of Israel and Judah were the "vineyard of the Lord Almighty . . . and the garden of his delight" (5:7). Jesus came as God's effective vine with branches that would continue producing God's kind of fruit as Jesus did.

The original language emphasized the "I" with a more accurate translation being "I **myself** am the true vine." The "vine" metaphor emphasized Jesus as the only One in whom authentic life existed for humans to tap. Minutes prior to the vine statement, Jesus declared, "I am the way and the truth and the life. No one comes to the Father except through me" (John 14:6).

God's true vine is not a political party, philosophy, palace, parent, palm reader, peddler, physician, psychologist, President, Prime Minister, Prince, or profession. It is not our plans, positions, principles, or powers, but only one person who declared, "I myself" (singular) am the true vine (singular), but you (plural) are the branches" (parenthesis mine). Every Christian has an intimately close connection to Jesus. God gave each of us His Spirit and grace-gifts to equip us to be effective branches whether we are nine years old or ninety, male or female, rich or poor, black or white, educated or illiterate, CEOs or day laborers, and so on.

Jesus communicated a reality that the agricultural people of his day instantly and clearly understood. Today the vine/branch metaphor may need an explanation for some who live in urbanized communities with more concrete than corn, more theaters than trees, more viruses than vines, and more bars than branches.

The invisible characteristics that course through the vine flow into the branches. Branches transport the invisible inner life of the vine into visible fruit that allows people to know the nature of the respective vine. The fruit which these human branches bare is not first of all other Christians, but the relational characteristics of Jesus that can draw people to Him, and through Him to God.

In this chapter we will slice into the vine in order to see what is inside it as revealed in John's Gospel that is to flow through Christians to produce corresponding fruit. Every chapter in John includes several characteristics, which would require a full-length book to explore. Consequently, we will be able to look at just a few in the next few pages.

Every Christian has an intimately close connection to Jesus. God gave each His Spirit and grace-gifts to equip us to be effective branches

The Word Fruit

"Word" is the first fruit mentioned in John, "In the beginning was the Word . . .He was with God in the beginning " (1:1-2). "Word" is from the Greek word *logos*, which meant communication that was full of meaning. Jesus was that *logos*-Word, "The Word became flesh and made his dwelling among us . . ." (John 1:14). Jesus was God's special delivery "mail." He was the Father's living letter that when opened and examined carefully revealed God (John 10:30; 14:9). **These same characteristics live in us**. Christians are God's on-going mail to be read and understood by all. But are we junk mail or first class mail? There are big differences between the two kinds of mail, such as the following:

First class mail is more personal. As first class mail, Christians need to view other people not as prospects to win, but as people to befriend. First class mail costs more. As first class mail, Christians need to stop asking first, "How much does that cost" but "How much is that needed?" First class mail travels faster. As first class mail, Christians need to be among the first, if not the first, to arrive when others experience disappointments, brokenness, hurts, and set backs, as well as delights, blessings, healings, and successes.

In New York, Marie Rothenberg's ex-husband was to take their 6-year son, David, to the Catskill Mountains for an outing. Instead, he excited David with, "We are going to Disneyland in California." After checking into a motel, the father gave David a sleeping pill, bought explosive fuel, poured it over his son's body, the bed, and the room, lit it, and raced out of the parking lot. The room literally exploded. Some people heard David's screams, ran into the room, and carried out the near-dead boy. The fire burned away David's skin, hair, eyebrows, eyelashes, nose, lips, fingers, and toes.

News about this tragedy was broadcast all over California, but no one knew the boy's identity. However, David's dad contacted Marie with the news that David might be a patient in the University of California, Irvine Hospital. She called the hospital and in excited desperation asked if David Rothenberg was a patient. At first, she got a negative answer, but the telephone receptionist was keen enough to transfer her call to David's room. The nurse there asked David, "Is you name, David?" There was enough movement that she said, "We aren't sure, but we may have your son here."

After Marie flew to Los Angeles, was taken to the hospital's burn center, and identified her son, the news media broke into all programs with the update. About twenty miles away, the Eastside Christian Church in Fullerton had just finished a jog-a-thon fundraiser to save the house of one of her members, Ken Curtis, who spent many months without income while recovering from first-degree burns sustained in an industrial fire. As Ken and his wife, Judy, were excitedly leaving the jog-a-thon, which saved their house from being repossessed, they turned on the radio to hear a reporter announce the identity of the boy and his mother. Judy remarked, "I know what she is going through and will continue to experience for months ahead." Ken replied, "And I know what David will go through. Let's go see if we can help." They stopped the car and prayed that they would be able to connect with Marie and befriend her. People called it a miracle that they got into David's room without being stopped by law officers, who were all over the area in uniform and plain clothes on the lookout for the father who had not yet been caught. Ken and Judy met Marie, told her their story, and offered their house to Marie, along with a vehicle and meals as long as she had need. For over a year they were Marie's extended family and closest friends in a strange land. Eventually both Marie and David became Christians out of the love of Ken, Judy, and the Eastside Church. That's first class mail with skin on.

How will people know what our God is like without getting a taste of what the vine offers by the fruit flowing through the branches? Some might answer, "Just read the Bible." However, most people on earth are illiterate. And many, if not most, who are educated in the Western world are biblically illiterate. But many have received special delivery "letters from Christ" they read and understand clearly. We Christians are God's letters wrapped with skin as affirmed by Paul to the Corinthian Christians, "You yourselves are our letter . . . known and read by everybody. You show that you are a letter from Christ, the result of our ministry, written not with ink but with the Spirit of the living God, not on tablets of stone but on tablets of human hearts" (2 Corinthians 3:2-3,). And a few paragraphs later, "So we are ambassadors for Christ, since God is making his appeal through us" (2 Corinthians 5:20 NRSV).

To be first class mail as Jesus was is one way to measure how close we are to being confirmed to the likeness of God, and thus becoming fully human in an inhuman world

The Creativity Fruit

Another characteristic inside the vine mentioned in John's Gospel is creativity, "through him all things were made; without him nothing was made that has been made" (John 1:3). God is innovative and that characteristic lives inside most people, whether Christians or not. But Christians should heighten, embrace, and enjoy creativity. Just consider the results of creativity since 1945—television, penicillin, frozen foods, plastic, split atoms, diversity of automatics (dishwashers, clothes washers, clothes dryers, transmissions, check-out counters, and so on), computers, cell-phones, microwave ovens, central air conditioning, satellite communications, a walk on the moon, a mechanical explorer on Mars that sends pictures to the earth, jet airplanes, super malls, the Interstate highway system, organ transplants, and so on.

During my lifetime, congregations have experienced significant changes, such as mega congregations, air conditioned buildings (no more hand fans in the pew racks with a message, "In case of death call _____(name) funeral home" as we sing, " "Because He lives I can face tomorrow," nurseries, large parking lots, family life centers, multi-staff generational ministers, audio-visual equipment, worship bands, multiple times and days for identical worship services, and so on.

However, sometimes people will split, because they did not get their way about some non-biblical traditions and their personal preferences, such as the order of worship, style of music, use or non-use of musical accompaniment (organ, piano, guitar, none, etc. What ever happened to the biblical harp?), times of the services, dress of the preacher (suit and tie, casual, robe), what to call the preacher (minister, pastor, evangelist, elder, father, brother, etc), selection of committee members, style of the worship building, and so on. We Christians need to embrace creativity in non-biblical matters with the following ABC responses:

- A— Act, don't argue.
- B— Build, don't blast.
- C— Create, don't criticize.
- D— Defend, don't defeat.
- E— Encourage, don't envy.
- F— Follow, don't fault.
- **G— Give, don't grumble.**
- H— Help, don't hinder.
- I— Invite, don't ignore.
- J— Join in, don't jeer it.
- K— Kneel, don't knock.
- L— Love, don't lambaste.
- M— Mend, don't mutter.
- N— Nurture, don't neglect.
- O— Obey, don't obstruct.
- P— Pray, don't pout.
- Q— Quicken, don't quit.
- R— Rescue, don't ridicule.
- T— Try it out, don't tear it down.
- U— Understand it, don't undercut it.
- V— Vindicate, don't plan vengeance.
- X— X-tend, don't x-cuse.
- Y— Yoke up, don't yell out.
- Z— Zeal for, don't zzzzzz from.

To be or to allow creativity in ways that advance God's purpose is one way to measure how close we are to being conformed to the likeness of God, and thus becoming fully human in an inhuman world

The Wide-Accepting-Heart Fruit

Another characteristic inside the vine is gleaned from chapters three and four in John's Gospel. Jesus reached out to two people who were socially and religiously opposites as described in the following:

Chapter three	Chapter four
A named person	An unnamed person
A male	A female
Jewish by birth	Multi-racial by birth
With status	With stigma
Moral	Immoral
Respected	Disrespected
Upper class	Lower class
Right religion	Wrong religion

Jesus' encounters with Nicodemus and the unnamed woman who had been married five times and was living with a man to whom she was not married illustrate that Jesus looks past the externals to see the real person whom God loves and for whom Jesus died. Inside the vine is a heart big enough to love all kinds of people; not just my kind or your kind, but the kinds we may not like or want; the kinds we love to hate, and hate to love. Inside the vine is the life that includes the excluded and the included; touches the untouchables and the touchables; sees the unseen and the seen; helps the helpless and the helpers; befriends the friendless and the friendly; delights the dull ones and the enlightened ones; accepts the unacceptable and the acceptable ones; and so on.

Every congregation needs to ask, "What kinds of people live in our area who do not have a clue that God sees them as precious persons, wants them to be in His family, and desires that someone will invite them to be His partners?" Every congregation should follow up the answer with ways to reach out to them by reaching in to the members and enlightening the eyes of their hearts, enlisting the emotions of their minds, and engaging the experiences of their lives. John's Gospel shows us how to bridge the gap between the differing people groups represented in John 3 and 4 by applying the same kind of love for them that God declared for all in His sacrificial human "bridge" that connected the man in chapter 3 and the woman in chapter 4 to God through Christ. John highlighted that bridge with this statement, "For God so loved the world that he gave his one and only Son. That whoever believes in him shall not perish but have eternal life" (John 3:16).

Inside the vine is the life that includes the excluded and the included, the untouchables and the touchables, helps the helpless and the helpers, befriends the friendless and the friendly, delights the dull ones and the enlightened ones; accepts the unacceptable and the acceptable ones.

Because of the limited space remaining in this chapter, we will fast forward toward the end of John's Gospel.

The Cross-bearing Fruit

Another characteristic inside the vine is cross bearing. "Carrying his own cross, he went out to the place of the Skull . . .Here they crucified him . . .." (John 19:17-18). This attribute is to flow through Christians. Jesus said to His disciples, "If anyone would come after me, he must deny himself and take up his cross and follow me" (Matthew 16:24). Jesus was not suggesting that Christians need to be literally executed on a physical cross, for that would empty this planet from God's family.

To live a cross-related life does not mean to live with our mate or go to work every day. It means to experience the dynamics that Jesus experienced in his cross-related life, which includes the following:

1. To give up our wishes for God's ways—"Not my will, but thine be done."
2. To be willing to stand alone for what is right.
3. To be willing to be rejected and forsaken by close friends.
4. To be willing to be embarrassed and mocked.
5. To be willing to not be believed.
6. To be willing to not be understood or appreciated.
7. To be willing to let others be chosen over you—Barabas over Jesus.
8. To be willing to make sacrifices to help others.
9. To be willing to stand up for others who are different from you—the thief on the cross next to Jesus.
10. To commit our lives to God, "Into your hands I commit. . .."

11. To be willing to stick to it and not look for a way out, "I could call twelve legions of angels."
12. To be willing not to respond with personal revenge.
13. To be willing to forgive those who mistreat you.
14. To be willing to apply the words of that song, "I Surrender all."

To live a cross-related life as Jesus did is one way to measure how close we are to being conformed to the likeness of God, and thus becoming fully human in an inhuman world

The Eternal Life Fruit

The last characteristic inside the vine is eternal life. Jesus rose from the tomb full of life. Eternal life refers to both the quality of life—what kind it is, and to the quantity of life—how long it is. The quality is God's kind of life modeled by Jesus. The quantity of life is everlasting. Both the quality and quantity live inside each branch. God's Spirit provides the quality (Galatians 5:22-24); and Jesus' death and resurrection provide the quantity, "I am the resurrection and the life. He who believes in me will live, even though he dies; and whoever lives and believes in me will never die" (John 11:25-26). The Christian's body will die physically, but the Christian will not. We all "will be changed. . . For the perishable must clothe itself with the imperishable, and the mortal with immortality. When the perishable has been clothed with the imperishable, and the mortal with immortality, then the saying that is written will come true. 'Death has been swallowed up in victory'. . . But thanks be to God! He gives us the victory through our Lord Jesus Christ. Therefore, my dear brothers, stand firm. Let nothing move you. Always give yourselves fully to the work of the Lord, because you know that your labor in the Lord is not in vain" (1 Corinthians 15: 51-58).

Because He lives, Christians can face tomorrow even though tomorrow might be the last day we take a breath on earth. With the eternality we have in Christ, we can face tomorrow with different ABCs than those not in Christ.

Death for the Christian

Is not	But is
A— Anxiety	Acceptance
B— A burden	A blessing
C— A curse	A celebration
D— A drudgery	A delight
E— An emptiness	An excitement
F— Frightening	Fulfillment
G— Gloom	Glory
H— Hell	Heaven
I— Incapacitation	Inauguration
J— A jolt	A joy
K— A kill	A kingdom
L— A lacking	A luxury
M— Misery	Majesty
N— Nasty	Noble
O— Offensive	Overcoming
P— Perishing	Promotion
Q— Quivering	Quietness
R— A retreat	A rest
S— Suffering	Salvation
T— In a tomb	Around the throne
U— Useless	Useful
V— As a victim	As a victor
X— "X-ing" you out	Xeroxing you into Christlikeness
W— Weakness	Wholesome
Y— A yelp	A yes
Z— Zero	Zeal

We have a glimpse of what is in store for us, "And I heard a loud voice from the throne saying, 'Now the dwelling of God is with men, and he will live with them. They will be his people, and God himself will be with them and be their God. He will wipe every tear from their eyes. There will be no more death or mourning or crying or pain, for the old order of things has passed away.' He who was seated on the throne said, 'I am making everything new. . . these words are trustworthy and true'"

(Revelation 21:3-4). Just think, no more lack of sleep, cosmetics to purchase, insurance premiums, cancer, headaches, backaches, prescriptions to fill, bills to pay, checkbooks to balance, accidents, murders, rapes, physical and mental abuse, retardation, strokes, paralysis, amputations, therapists, credit cards, debts, time clocks to punch, getting behind in work, stress, getting fired, loneliness, getting older and showing it by the day, and so on.

That kind of future is ahead of us, but are there physical benefits on this side of physical death?

We will introduce some of them in the next chapter.

12

How Then Can We Feel?

Spiritual Health and Physical Health

Spiritual development does not just affect our spiritual health, but can also affect our physical well-being. Our life on earth is a temporary stopover. It is biblically compared to a mist that appears for a little while (James 4:14); to a breath (Job 7:7); to smoke that vanishes (Psalm 102:3); to a withering flower and a fleeting shadow (Job 14:2); to dust (Psalm 103:14); and to grass that is here in the morning, but gone by evening (Psalm 90:5-6). The temporariness of our earthly nature does not mean we were physically put together with inferior material. Far from it, for we are God's creative work, which is wonderful (Psalm 139:14). We humans are the result of God artful design (Ephesians 2:10).

What the manufacturer's guide is for our products the "Godufacturer's Guide", the Bible, is to our personhood. The contents equip us to better understand the reality of who we are and how to take care of who we are.

Scientific research is catching up with scriptural revelations about what affects our physical well-being. What are considered to be revolutionary data from research were old declarations from revelation, which have easily been overlooked.

How Then Can We Feel?

In a 2002 article published in the *Journal of the American Medical Association*, Harold Koeniq, M.D. at Duke University, reported that medical science has conducted 724 studies about the relationship of religion to physical health with about two thirds showing a positive association between religious activities and better health. Since 2002, research connecting physical health to spirituality has mushroomed at such a rapid pace that it is being viewed as one of the recent breakthroughs in the medical field. Several medical schools have added a psychoneuroimmunological department that researches religious affects on human physiology. For instance, Andrew Newberg, M.D., a researcher in Nuclear Medicine at the University of Pennsylvania, is doing pioneering work in neurotheology, which integrates neuro science with religion. By using positive-emission topography and magnetic imagining (MRI), he is able to notice and record changes in the brain as a person engages in religious activities. Consequently, the brain can release various chemicals that affect healing. Newberg is researching how spiritual practices affect the release of those chemicals that hastens healing as well protects against diseases.

Another example of the growing interest in the relationship of spirituality to healing is the work of Rachel Remen, M.D., who developed "The Healer's Art" course at the University of California, San Francisco. This course stresses the balance of physicians' caring relationship with their competent medical techniques. She affirms that stressing only professionalism in medical schools has caused potential physicians to disown and oppress certain parts of their own humanity. According to Dr. Remen, emphasizing only professional techniques neglects helping people with the doctor's humanity in ways techniques cannot. The lack of balancing professional techniques with the physician's touch has been lacking in both medical and ministerial schools. Both schools need Remen's concepts in "The Art of Healing" course, which Jesus modeled by balancing His compassion with His competence. Her course is now being taught in nearly thirty different medical schools. Shouldn't the concepts also be taught in every ministerial school and in every congregation for developing people to become fully human living in an inhuman world?

Presently 70% of medical schools in this country offer at least one course in spirituality. The Continuing Education Department at Harvard University's Medical School offers different courses in its popular

"Spirituality and Healing" track. In that track, Harvard teaches that there is a live-in pharmacy inside the human brain to which we send prescriptions by our attitudes and actions, which the brain will always fill. Some of those prescriptions are therapeutic that aids healing, and some are toxic that inhibits healing. That track teaches that a lot of illness result from a dis-ease-ment (thus disease), which is related to what is going on in a person's life that is out of balance. Seventy-four percent of complaints in a physician's office can be traced to psychosocial origins.

Our Internal Pharmacy

Cardiologist Herbert Benson at Harvard teaches that the medical field is built on the three-legged stool of medicine, surgery, and self-help. The self-help is the inner healer inside of us with the brain functioning as a pharmaceutical dispensary with a wide rage of chemicals and substances stored in the brain or elsewhere in the body that can be released by "a call" from the brain. God designed us with our own inner physician to cooperate with external physicians. Neither "physician" should ignore the existence and services of the other one.

Research affirms that attitudes, beliefs, activities, and emotions ranging from love and compassion to fear and anger can trigger chain reactions that affect the activity of every cell and organic system in the body. Every system in the human body has receptors that receive the prescriptions sent or ordered from the brain. The condition of our physical body is partly the outward manifestation of what is going on in the mind-body interdependence and interaction. No wonder God inspired Paul to write, "be transformed by the renewing of your mind" (Romans 12:2). God knew exactly how we were designed, and how our internal physician can help or harm us.

Most of God's built-in healing benefits reduce stress. God knew we would live in a stress-filled world and the physical changes that stress triggers. According to cardiologist Herbert Benson, 60-90% of visits to a physician's office are stress related. The physical affects of stress are legion. Stress produces hormonal imbalance and killer cells called T-Lymphocytes and Macrophages, which weaken our internal fight against disease. Stress increases blood pressure, the heart rate, cholesterol level and plaques in the arteries. Stress contributes to stomach and intestinal disorders, headaches, muscle tightening, backaches, and heart arrhythmia. Stress decreases the level of potassium, calcium, and cortisol, which can prevent the formation of new immune cells. Stress is related to many other physical disorders as well. If all the above happened at once, just a minor stress could instantly kill us. Medical science also reports that stress can trigger many different diseases, such as coronary heart, asthma, ulcerative colitis, rheumatoid arthritis, hypertension, strokes, gastrointestinal problems, and cancer.

Research on the relationship of spirituality and healing is expanding so rapidly that any reported results are outdated by the time they are published. We are at the cutting edge of catching up to some specific realities summarized with "physical training is of some value, but godliness has value for all things holding promise for both the present life and the life to come" (1 Timothy 4:8). Below are some recent scientific revolutionary discoveries with their collateral revelational declarations in the Bible:

The Tranquility Factor

Revolutionary Discovery. Positive thinking sends a therapeutic "prescription" to the brain's pharmacy that releases into every cell valium-like substances, such as peptides, endorphins, and encephalins which produce feelings of peace that help us to rest, to adapt to situations, and hastens the healing process.

Carl Simonton, M.D., an internationally acclaimed oncologist and medical researcher, notes that cancer is often an indication of problems in a person's life aggravated or compounded by a series of stresses six to eight months prior to the appearance of the cancer. According to Simonton, stress triggers a set of physiological responses that suppress the body's natural defenses making it more susceptible to produce abnormal cells. Simonton believes the purpose of providing health care is to bring harmony within patients. Bernie Siegel, M.D. also believes that the primary task of physicians is to help patients achieve a peace of mind (*Love, Medicine, & Miracles*).

Revelational Declarations. "A heart at peace gives life to the body" (Proverbs 14:30). Jesus declared, "Peace I leave with you" (John 14:27). Paul wrote that positive thinking, which comes through faith and hope in Christ and is gifted by the Holy Spirit produces a tranquility that surpasses understanding (Philippians 4:4-9).

The Laughter Factor

Revolutionary Discovery. Laughter releases catecholamine that strengthens the immune system. The muscles of the chest, abdomen, and face get a workout. Laughter relaxes the diaphragm, exercises the lungs, tunes up the cardiovascular system, lowers blood pressure, increases the oxygen exchange, decreases the heart rate, and stimulates beta-endorphins, which are feel-good brain chemicals.

Revelational Declaration. "A cheerful heart is good medicine" (Proverbs 17:22). Literally "causes good healing". My paraphrase— "Laughter is good medicine").

The Optimism Factor

Revolutionary Discoveries. A 13-year study of 2,832 people found that those who were pessimists were 1Ω times more likely to die of heart disease than those who were optimists. A Mayo Clinic study revealed that pessimists have a 19% greater likelihood of premature death than optimists. George Vallint, M.D., Pathologist at Cambridge Hospital in Cambridge, Massachusetts, did a study which revealed that alcohol and tobacco use, obesity, and the life span of parents were not as significant in determining a person's physical well-being and longevity as the person's positive mental state. A 27-year study from Duke University found that people with high levels of negativism and low self-esteem were 70% more likely to die from a heart attack.

Revelational Declarations. "Hope deferred makes the heart sick" (Proverbs 13:12). God "has given us new birth into a living hope through the resurrection of Jesus Christ from the dead" (1 Peter 1:3). Hope is "an anchor for the soul" (Hebrews 6:19).

The Faith Factor

Revolutionary Discoveries. Faith can help to both prevent and heal diseases. A study of 91,999 people living in Washington County, Maryland discovered those with faith who attended church once or more a week experienced lower cases of certain diseases, such as a 50% reduction in coronary disease, 56% less instances of emphysema, 74% reduction in cirrhosis of the liver, and fewer pulmonary diseases. Other studies have affirmed the health benefits of faith to healing (See *Faith is Good Medicine* by medical researcher, Dale Matthews, M. D.). Barry Wyke, M. D., a member of the Royal College of Surgeons in London, shared documentary proof that positive physical changes occur when people believe they are going to get well.

Revelational Declarations. Jesus said to one person, "Your faith has healed you" (Luke 8:48); and to another, "According to your faith, it will be done to you" (Matthew 9:29). Perhaps that is a collateral benefit to the biblical admonition, "Let us not give up meeting together, as some are in the habit of doing, but let us encourage one another—and all the more as you see the Day approaching" (Hebrews 10:25).

The Tongue Factor

Revolutionary Discovery. Research reveals that we can talk ourselves into a dis-ease-ment. Negative words from other people toward us can make us physically ill, while positive words can hasten recovery from a sickness. A physician's words and tone of voice can help or hinder healing. Harvard University Medical School teaches the importance of what a physician says and how he says it. In some cases the doctor's mouth may be as important as the medicine.

Revelational Declarations. "Words of a gossip are like choice morsels; they go down to a person's inmost parts" (Proverbs 18:8). "Pleasant words are a honeycomb, sweet to the soul and healing to the bones" (Proverbs 16:24). Honeycomb was used for medicine in those days. "The tongue has the power of life and death" (Proverbs 18:21). The tongue sets in motion a cycle that affects us holistically (James 3: 6).

The Friendship Factor.

Revolutionary Discovery. Those with several friends have fewer diseases and heal faster than those who do not. For over 50 years researchers studied the people who lived in Roseto, Pennsylvania. In spite of many high risk factors for heart disease and diabetes, they had a much lower rate of those diseases with a much lower mortality rate than residents in the surrounding area. Research concluded their good health was due primarily to a close cohesive relationship with one another. The California Mental Health Department produced a little booklet titled, "Friends Can Be Good Medicine" with supporting data that friendships provide a level of protection against cancer, heart, cerebral, vascular, and other diseases. The booklet reported a 9-year study of California's Alameda County, which discovered that people with few ties to others had two to five times the death rate of those who had more ties, and concluded that connection with others was more important to impacting health than smoking, drinking, exercising, or diet. The University of Texas Medical School concluded that those without a support group experienced a fourfold increase of dying six month after surgery than those with a support group.

Revelational Declarations. The church is to be a support group that crosses all kinds of sociological categories, so people can have close connections to God and others. Christians are to live with one another with complementation, not competition as living stones in the same temple, branches in the same vine, and children in the same family. The Bible consistently stresses connectional responsibilities to each other that include all the "one anothers" in the New Testament, such as love, be devoted to, give preference to, don't condemn, build up, be of the same mind with, accept, admonish (put sense into another's way of thinking), teach, wait for, have the same care for, serve, don't bite and devour, don't be envious, forbear (put up with), be kind to, speak to, submit to, don't lie to, forgive, abound in love for, comfort, encourage, live in peace with, seek what is good for, stimulate to love and good deeds, don't complain against, confess to, pray for, love from the heart, be hospitable to, use gifts for, be humble toward, fellowship with, and regard one another as more important than self.

It is possible that some troubles in a congregation have their origin in one or more of the above not being applied. When we get to heaven, we may be shocked to learn how much more spiritually and physically healthy a congregation and her members would have been with lower relational problems and lower medical bills were the "one anothers" taught and modeled as a basic evidence of active Christianity. **To do the one another's is one way to measure how close we are getting to being conformed to the likeness of God, and thus becoming fully human in an inhuman world.**

The Anger Factor

Revolutionary Discovery. Medical science reveals that chronic anger triggers an autonomic response in which the body attacks itself. Hanging on to anger increases plaques in the arteries, narrows the arteries, inhibits nerve signals that regulate the heart rhythm, elevates blood pressure, weakens the immune system, lowers resistance to diseases, tightens muscles, increases cholesterol, and negatively affects the central nervous system. A Harvard University study of 1600 heart attack patients revealed that the risk of an attack doubles during or after an episode of anger. Twenty to twenty-five percent of people who died suddenly from cardiac arrest had been angry shortly before the deadly event.

Revelational Declarations. "In your anger do not sin. Do not let the sun go down while you are still angry" (Ephesians 4:26). "Get rid of all bitterness, rage, and anger. . ." (Ephesians 4:30).

The Meditation Factor

Revolutionary Discovery. Medical research affirms that positive meditation bolsters the human immune responses, improves white blood cell responses, hastens the healing of diseases, decreases metabolism, lowers blood pressure, lowers the heart rate, relaxes muscles, reduces the level of stress hormones, and reduces the rate of biological aging.

Revelational Declarations. Old Testament leaders got away to meditate (Genesis 24:63). The Psalmist wrote that one way to reduce anger is to meditate (Psalm 4:4). Christian meditation should be upon God's ways (Psalm 119:15), God's Word, (Psalm 119:97), God's promises (Psalm 119:148), and God's works (Psalms 145:5), and a host of other aspects related to our triune God.

The Forgiving Factor

Revolutionary Discovery. Medical science has documented several health benefits of forgiving, which include immediate improvement in the cardiovascular, muscular, and nervous systems. Studies report that forgiving decreases anxiety, lessens depression, lowers stress, increases inner joy, improves self-esteem, improves grief recovery, increases the capacity to love, and heightens a person's readiness to serve others. Medical research also reveals the negative physical results of holding grudges. Doing so increases heart rate, tightens muscles, raises blood pressure, weakens the immune system, heightens the risk factor for heart attacks, interferes with sleep, and is associated with higher incidences of cancer and cardiovascular diseases.

Revelational Declaration. God's Word repeatedly includes forgiving others as part of being a Christian (Matthew 6:12-15; 18:21-15; John 20:23; 2 Corinthians 2:7; Ephesians 4:32; Colossians 3:13).

I am convinced that everything God revealed for us to believe and to practice is first of all for our holistic well-being—spiritually, socially, and physically, each of which interacts and affects the other. To neglect one is to weaken the other. To support one is to build up the other. We were holistically created by the holistic God who is the model of unity with diversity within the Trinity. He desires that we become relationally whole as He is. Paul got at that when he wrote, "May God himself, the God of peace, sanctify you through and through. May your whole spirit, soul and body be kept blameless at the coming of our Lord Jesus Christ" (1 Thessalonians 5:23).

We can do with the "Godufacturer's Guide" what we do with a manufacturer's guide. We can take it or leave it. We can follow it or neglect it. But to walk away from it is to hurt our well-being in all aspects of living. On the other hand, to follow our Designer is to the take hold of life and have it more abundantly.

How Then Can We Feel?

To follow our Designer as Jesus did is one way to measure how close we are getting to being conformed to the likeness of God, and thus becoming fully human living in an inhuman world

But can we really be whole through and through? Can we really become like Christ before we get to heaven? Or is it possible that we are chasing after the wind, but will never catch it?

To that we will address in the next chapter.

13

Before We Get To Heaven, We Can Become Like Him

A Positive Goal

God did not fail when He created various plants according to their kinds (Genesis 1:11-12). God did not fail when He designed sea life, birds, and every creature that crawls on the ground according to their kinds (Genesis 1:20-21). God did not fail when He produced livestock and wild animals according to their kinds (Genesis 1:24-25). And God did not fail when He announced, "Let us make humankind in our image, according to our likeness" (Genesis 1:26, NRSV). Each non-human kind of life functioned according to its created nature. Humankind also functioned according to God's nature until Adam and Eve voluntarily decided to prioritize pleasing self rather than God (Genesis 3:6).

As God did not falter in His designed creation, so He was not deficient in His designed goal for humans on earth, ". . . to be conformed to the likeness of his Son" (Romans 8:29). Becoming like Christ may be the most needed, but yet the most neglected issue in the Church today. Some teach that reaching such a goal is not possible this side of heaven. However, it is wrong to contradict any one of the members of the Trinity. When Peter contradicted Jesus, He responded with, "Get behind me, Satan! You are a stumbling block to me; you do not have in mind the things of God, but the things of man" (Matthew 16:22-23).

Becoming like Christ may be the most needed, but yet the most neglected issue in the Church today

Positive Steps

God not only announced His goal for us, but also revealed how we could reach it. The first step is to experience a new creation in Christ (2 Corinthians 5:17) that recycles us to be like God, "created to be like God in true righteousness [right relationships] and holiness [committed to our new nature]" (Ephesians 4:24. Brackets mine). God did that by putting His own *sperma* in us so we could participate in His nature by drawing from His life in us (1 John 3:9; 3:24; Ephesians 2:22; 2 Peter 1:4). The reality of that first step rests upon our choice to enter into a new relationship with God through Christ.

The second step for being conformed into the likeness of Christ is commit self to grow up according to His kind through progressive transformation that involves putting off old preferences and practices and putting on new ones (Ephesians 4:20-24; 1 Peter 2:1-3; 2 Peter 1:5-11; Romans 12:1-21; Philippians 2:1-5), which is summed up by Paul, "Since, then, you have been raised with Christ . . .set your minds on things above, not on earthly things . . . Put to death, therefore, whatever belongs to your earthly nature . . .and put on the new self, which is being renewed in knowledge in the image of its Creator" (Colossians 3:1-10). Progressive transformation is possible if we do not quench God's Spirit in us (Ephesians 5:19), but instead keep in step with His Spirit (Galatians 5:25), because "where the Spirit of the Lord is, there is freedom. And we, who with unveiled faces all reflect the Lord's glory [character], are being transformed into his likeness with ever-increasing glory [character], which comes from the Lord, who is the Spirit" (2 Corinthians 3:17-18. Brackets mine.).

Becoming Like Christ

We **can** become like Him on earth before we get to heaven.

Becoming like Christ is about becoming an earthly child of God who pleases Him.

Becoming like Christ is about being a member in the body of Christ who helps give the Head a healthy functioning body.

Becoming like Christ is about the on-going presence of Christ living in us and through us in the midst of on-going perversions surrounding us.

Becoming like Christ is about being people of "lovalism" instead of legalism.

Becoming like Christ is about being all we were meant to be.

Becoming like Christ is about keeping all we are; all we think; all we do; and all we do not do in step with the Father, the Son, and the Holy Spirit.

Becoming like Christ is not only about being saved by His death, but is also about being "much more . . . shall we be saved (be whole) through his life" living in us (Romans 5:10, parenthesis mine).

Becoming like Christ is to function according to our created and recreated kind in the image and likeness of God.

Becoming like Christ is being naturally human, because it squares with our original created nature.

Becoming like Christ is to forgive the way He did.

Becoming like Christ is to please the Father the way He did.

Becoming like Christ is to live the cross-related life the way He did.

Becoming like Christ is to be generous with our time and money.

Becoming like Christ is to not yield to temptations the way He did not.

Becoming like Christ is to let all His relational characteristics flow through us as branches extending the Vine's life throughout the world.

Becoming like Christ is to give Him our big "D" death and take on his big "L" life.

Becoming like Christ is to not be disconnected from the functions of our physical bodies, but to offer mind, soul, and body as members of His new body on earth.

Becoming like Christ is to be open to all kinds of people including those we might at one time loved to hate and hated to love.

Becoming like Christ is to serve and support His Church locally and globally.

Becoming like Christ is about keeping in step with the Holy Spirit.

Becoming like Christ is to become a friend of sinners.

Becoming like Christ is to be transformed from being inhuman to be becoming fully human living in an inhuman world.

The reason the above looks so distance and difficult is because it is a lifestyle that challenges the influential models in our culture.

Progressive transformation is possible if we do not quench God's Spirit, but instead keep in step with the Spirit

Positive Assessment

All aspects of a congregation's programs and ministries are to be measured not only by evangelizing people, but also by equipping new members to grow up into Christlikeness. It usually takes much more thought, energy, intentionality, hard work, and evaluative assessments to mature present Christians than it does to produce new ones.

A two-faceted measure of a congregation's maturity is whether or not all kinds of people in the surrounding area are being blessed by members, and similarly if the mission, support, and outreach of a congregation include a ministry to all kinds of different categories of people locally and globally (Genesis 12:2-3; Acts 3:24-25; Galatians 3:8; John 3:16; Matthew 28-19-20).

It does not take much to physically grow old in our technological culture. We can physically grow old without eating on our own through IV drips and without breathing on our own through ventilators. But it takes a lot to grow up to become a mature adult. Collaterally, it does not take much to spiritually grow old as a Christian, but it takes a lot to become a spiritually mature Christian, who models Christlikeness. If that does not happen, it will not be because it is impossible, but because of our personal choices. Spiritual maturity will not happen if we adopt Peter Pan's line, "I won't grow up. I won't grow up." And it will not happen if we cave in to that line in a western song, "Just rollin' along drifting like the tumble weed." And it will not happen if we accept and pass on to others the line from some Christian teaching, "It's not possible to become like Christ on this side of heaven."

All aspects of a congregation's programs and ministries are to be measured not only by evangelizing people, but also by equipping new members to grow up into Christlikeness

As it **is** possible to mature physically, so it **is** possible to mature spiritually. The Greek word *teleios* is sometimes translated as "perfect." *Teleios* describes something or someone that has reached an intended goal. When used about a person it described someone who was mature. Every time it is used in the New Testament, it would be better to translate it as "mature."

Positive Provisions

In His "Godufactured Guide" God communicated His intention for us to keep advancing toward the maturity described as being conformed to the likeness of Christ (Romans 8:29). Here are just a few of His inspired enlightenments with that in mind:

- "A student is not above his teacher, but everyone who is fully trained will be like his teacher" (Luke 6:40). Jesus gave no hint that it would not be possible to be like Him.
- God gifted the Church with leaders "to prepare God's people for works of service, so that the body of Christ may be built up until we all reach unity in the faith and in the knowledge of the Son of God and become mature, attaining to the whole measure of the fullness of Christ" (Ephesians 4:9-13). There is no hint that it is not possible to become mature to the fullness of Christ.
- "All Scripture is God breathed and is useful for teaching, rebuking, correcting and training in righteousness so that the man of God may be thoroughly equipped for every good work" (2 Timothy 3:16-17). There is no hint that we cannot be thoroughly equipped.

- "Christ in you, the hope of glory [character]. It is he whom we proclaim, warning everyone and teaching everyone in all wisdom **so that we may present everyone mature in Christ.** For this I toil and struggle with all the energy that he powerfully inspires within me" (Colossians 1:27-29 NRSV. Brackets and bold mine). Paul gave no hint that it would not be possible for people to mature.

Positive Attitudes

Scripture affirms the possibility of reaching maturity in the following texts:

- "All of us who are mature should take such a view of things. . . .Only let us live up to what we have already attained" (Philippians 3:15-16). There is no hint that Paul lied about some people were already mature. And by using "us" admitted his own maturity.
- "Be imitators of me, just as I also am of Christ" (1 Corinthians 11:1, NASB). There is no hint that we cannot mature to the level of imitating Christ and God, as Paul did. See also Ephesians 5:1-2.
- ". . . and it is no longer I who live, but it is Christ who lives in me. And the life I now live in the flesh I live by faith in the Son of God, who loved me and gave himself for me" (Galatians 2:20). There is no hint that others cannot live like Christ who lives in them.
- "Whoever claims to live in him must walk as Jesus did" (1 John 2:6). There is no hint that we cannot do that.
- "Your attitude should be the same as that of Christ Jesus" (Philippians 2:5). There is no hint that we have to die and get to heaven first in order to do that.
- "Since we live by the Spirit, let us keep in step with the Spirit" (Galatians 5:25). There is no hint that we have to wait for streets of gold to keep in step with the Spirit. We can do it here with mud up to our ankles.

- "Like newborn babes crave pure spiritual milk, so that by it you may grow up in your salvation" (1 Peter 2:2). There is no hint that growing up spiritually is not possible.
- "In fact, though by this time you ought to be teachers, you need someone to teach you the elementary truths of God's word all over again. You need milk, not solid food! Anyone who lives on milk, being still an infant, is not acquainted with the teaching about righteousness. But solid food is for the mature, who by constant use have trained themselves to distinguish good from evil. Therefore let us leave the elementary teaching about Christ and go on to maturity. . .And God permitting, we will do so" (Hebrews 5:12-6-3). There is no hint that God will not permit us to go on to maturity. But it is clear that people have not given themselves permission to mature.

What God taught should be done, and what He equipped us to do can be done. It is past time for people to quit thinking it cannot be done. After all, growing up into Christlikeness captures the significance of what it means to be a Christian and a disciple of Christ.

What God taught should be done, and what He equipped us to do can be done

Positive Discipleship

In the Greek New Testament, the word Christian is "Christ" with an *ianos* ending—*Christianos*. Those letters attached to a person's name, title, or position described a person who was totally devoted to the person who held that title or position. Thus a Caesarianos was a person devoted to live for, to support, and to advance Caesar's position, programs, and purposes. Such a person was a Caesar fanatic—his fan, and considered it an honor to belong to Caesar, to be identified as one of Caesar's, and to be Caesar's cheerleading representative. "Christian" is not a weak label for a person who simply gives lip service to believing in Christ, but it is a strong label for one who is attached to Christ, belongs to Christ, and lives to support and to advance Christ's position, programs, and purpose.

"Christian" describes anyone who lives as Christ's cheerleading representative—His ambassador. We have no right to dilute that meaning for today's culture. The parallel label of a Christian in Jesus' day was a "disciple of Christ."

The basic description of a disciple is a "student—a learner." However, a disciple in Jesus' day was far different from today's students and learners. A disciple in Jesus' day referred to someone who was bonded to another person for the purpose of becoming like that other one. A disciple assimilates the attitudes and actions of the mentor—to imitate or to mimic the other one. Thus to be a disciple of Christ calls for unconditionally surrendering one's independent lifestyle to the lifestyle of Jesus. To be invited to be Jesus' disciple is a call to be fanatically devoted to Him in order to be transformed into His character.

The Holy Spirit in Jesus equipped Him with the Father's character (glory) that enabled Him to be fully human in an inhuman world. The same Holy Spirit is inside each person and equips each one with the same character (glory) of God that enables us to be fully human in an inhuman world. God's eternal life enters from the outside into our inside so we will live from the inside out in ways that extend His presence throughout the world.

A "disciple" in Jesus' day referred to someone who bonded to another person for the purpose of becoming like that other one. Being a disciple of Christ calls for unconditionally surrendering one's independent lifestyle to the lifestyle of Jesus

Three questions that are contemporary in any culture are these:

- Do we really want to be so bonded to Jesus that we become His loyal, devoted, and fanatic cheerleading representatives—His ambassadors on earth who practice the principles of Christ?
- Do we really want to be identified with the minority instead of with the majority (Matthew 7:13-14)?
- Does the Church really want to live the fullness of the Life already given to it as revealed by Paul, "And God placed all things under

his feet and appointed him to be head over everything for the church, which is his body, **the fullness of him who fills everything in every way**" (Ephesians 1:22-23. Bold print mine)?

If a congregation really wants to advance all members toward the likeness of Christ, which she inherited, then she needs to analyze what she is doing to integrate this into her mission, ministry, and methods.

This also requires commitment to God and from Satan described in the next chapter.

14

How Shall We Then Commit?

On one hand, Paul declared that his mission was to bring salvation to all kinds of people not only through preaching, but also through relationships, "Though I am free . . .I make myself a slave to everyone, to win as many as possible. To the Jews I became like a Jew, to win the Jews. To those under the law I became like one under the law (though I myself am not under the law), so as to win those under the law. To those not having the law I became like one not having the law (though I am not free from God's law but am under Christ's), so as to win those not having the law. To the weak I became weak, to win the weak. I have become all things to all men so that by all possible means I might save some" (1 Corinthians 9:19-22).

On the other hand, Paul declared that his mission was also to mature those saved, "To them God chose to make known how great among the Gentiles are the riches of the glory [character] of this mystery [strategy], which is Christ in you the hope of glory [character]. It is he whom we proclaim, warning everyone and teaching everyone in all wisdom, **so that we may present everyone mature in Christ**. For this I toil and struggle with all the energy that he powerfully inspires within me" (Colossians 1:27-29 NRSV. Bold and brackets mine).

We cannot keep those two missions together in tandem by being independent Christians. The more we are like Christ, the more we will be able to win others to Him. "Christ in you the hope of glory [character]" refers to Christians who live Christ-like lives through their diverse experiences, such as through wage-earning employments, volunteer services, families, leisure, hobbies, neighborhoods, clubs, committees, churches, and so on. Wherever Christians are they are God's only hope that His character will be in all those places and situations. That is our mission, which calls for maturity in Christ and not just membership in a congregation.

The mission of Christian higher education and the Church should be no less than that declared and demonstrated by Paul, and modeled and commissioned by Jesus, "Go therefore and **make disciples** of all nations [ethnic groups], baptizing them in the name of the Father and of the Son and of the Holy Spirit [win them], and **teaching them to obey everything** that I have commanded you [help mature them]. And remember, I am with you always, to the end of the age" (Matthew 28:19-20, NRSV. Bold and brackets mine).

Growing old is easy, but growing up is not. We are not to keep drinking spiritual milk and crawling as infants, but are to resolve to continually digest spiritual meat and to walk, run, leap, and climb heights as mature Christians filled with God's Spirit (Ephesians 5:18), able to evangelize sinners outside of Christ, and to edify saints in Christ so they can enjoy being fully human in an inhuman world.

We are not to keep drinking spiritual milk and crawling as infants, but are to resolve to continually digest spiritual meat and to walk, run, leap, and climb heights as mature Christians filled with God's Spirit

What kind of commitments can help us stay on track? The first one is to stay committed to our connection to Christ while staying in a world that dangles many distractions in front of us.

My favorite story about that kind of commitment comes from a true story about John Blanchard, a World War II lieutenant stationed in Florida. Lt. Blanchard checked a book out of the library, started reading it, noticed handwritten notes in the margins, and was impressed by the insights of the

How Shall We Then Commit?

note taker. Turning to the inside cover, he saw a woman's name and address written in the same handwriting as the marginal notes. Blanchard decided to write her a note to express how much he appreciated her written comments.

That began a long period of exchanging letters before Blanchard was shipped overseas. The exchanges continued to the place that Blanchard thought he might be falling in love with his correspondent. So he asked for her picture. She replied with something like this, "If you think you are falling in love with me, it should not matter how I look, should it?" He decided not to press for her picture, and he did not send her one of him.

After the war, they decided to meet at Grand Central station in New York City. To recognize each other, she would be wearing a large red rose, and he would be in his uniform holding that book. As the train stopped, Lt. Blanchard stood up, straightened his uniform, and held the book so it could be easily seen. Then he saw a beautiful blond with a shapely knit mint colored dress coming toward him. On a score of 1 to 10, she was at least a 1,500. But she was not wearing a red rose. However, she walked right up to him, winked, and said in a soft voice, "Going my way, soldier?" Everything in him wanted to say, "You bet, babe, I am going your way right now!" But he remembered the commitment to his pen pal, so let the alluringly attractive beauty pass by without his response.

Then he saw another woman coming toward him with the big red rose pinned on her dress. She was graying, short, a bit stooped over, and stocky. On a score of 1 to 10, she was about a minus 5. He knew this would not be a romance, but she had been and could continue to be a good friend. So he walked up to her and said, "I am Lieutenant John Blanchard. May I take you out to dinner?" That short stocky woman looked up at him and replied, "Soldier, I have no idea what this is all about. But just before the train stopped that beautiful blond up ahead with that gorgeous knit mint dress took a rose off her dress, pinned it on mine, and said, 'If a tall Lieutenant in his uniform carrying a book asks you out to dinner, tell him that I am waiting for him at the restaurant just across the street at a corner table with a candle lit.'" A standing ovation for you, John Blanchard, for that's real commitment.

How about our commitment to Christ? Would it get a standing ovation from heaven? There is so much in this world that looks like a 1,500 on a score of 1 to 10. Many times substitutes approach us with a wink and an invitation, "Going my way, friend?" Will we let them pass right by as we remember our commitment to Christ? And then, while still standing seemingly alone, there He comes looking tired, fatigued, beaten up, with blood flowing from His side, hands, and feet. Keeping our focus glued on Him, we come to His side with, "I want to take you with me from now on wherever you go and be your partner in whatever you do. I am proud to be your disciple and to be seen with you."

Our commitment to Christ needs to be linked to a corresponding commitment to His on-going body, the Church—His only family on earth

It takes planned intentionality to not let what the world dangles distract us from following Christ. However, we must not think that what the world dangles is on a score of 1,500 while Christ's score is minus 5. Oh no! Christ is beyond 1,500. He is matchless, awesome, beautiful, outstanding, precious, brilliant, and appealing.

Commitment to Christ needs to be linked to a corresponding commitment to His on-going body, the Church—His only family on earth. That commitment can sound something like this:

> I am a part of the Church of the unashamed. I have Holy Spirit power. The die has been cast. I've stepped over the line. I am a disciple of Christ. I won't look back, let up, slow down, back away, or be still. My past is redeemed. My present makes sense, and my future is secure. I am finished with drinking the milk of infants and crawling like a spiritual baby. I am done with staying the way I have been. I will continually grow up toward the likeness of Christ.
>
> I am done with low living, small planning, smooth knees, colorless dreams, tame visions, mundane talking, stingy giving, dwarfed goals, prayerless days, workaholic, busyaholic and goaholic schedules. I will no longer cling to grudges, stay where the activities and noise that drown out Christ, be addicted to the TV that squeezes out the Father, and neglect spiritual disciplines that shuts out the Holy Spirit.
>
> I no longer need pre-eminence, prosperity, position, promotions, or popularity. I don't have to be right, first, tops, recognized, praised, regarded, or rewarded. I live in the Father's Son, love by the Father's compassion, and keep in step with God's Spirit.

How Shall We Then Commit?

My goal is to be like Him. My road is narrow. My way is rough, and my companions may be few. But my "Godufactured Guide" is reliable, and my mission is clear. I cannot be bought, compromised, detoured, lured away, turned back, diluted, or delayed. I will not flinch in the face of sacrifice, hesitate in the presence of adversity, negotiate at the table of the enemy, ponder at the pool of popularity, or meander in the maze of mediocrity.

I won't give up, let up, or slow up till I have become like Christ. I am a disciple of Him. And when He comes to get His own, He'll have no problem recognizing me, for He will see Himself in my face, in my smile, in my life, in my love, and in all those who have been drawn to Him, the Vine, through His fruit that flows through me.

That kind of commitment needs to be linked to a commitment against Satan that can sound something like this:

> Satan, listen up, listen now, and listen well! We're the Church of the living God. We're bought with blood, charged with power, indwelt with His Spirit, immune from destruction, and destined for victory.
>
> We will not fear your foolishness, run from your roaring, fold under your fire, buckle under your barking, abandon your attacks, be lulled by your likes, be vulnerable to your viciousness, be scattered by your schemes, or be derailed by your deceptions.
>
> We are a part of the company of the committed, the crowd of the courageous, the crew of the commissioned, the army of the Almighty, the fleet of the fighters, the battalion of the believers, the regiment of the redeemed, the division of the devoted, the platoon of the powerful, the squadron of the Savior, and the ship of the Son.
>
> Satan, we are united together and will stand firm against you with the blessings in the Bible, the character of the Christ, the defense of Deity, the energy of the Emmanuel, the faith in the Father, the gifts of God, the help of the Head, the impassion of the Immortal, the joy of Jesus, the kick of the King, the love of the Lord, the might of the Master, the optimism of the Omnipotent, the power of Providence, the resolve of the Rock, the sword of the Spirit, the tactics of the Trinity, the victory of the Victorious, the way of the Lord, and the zeal of Zion.
>
> Satan, the clock is running out for you! We wait for our consummation and your condemnation, our reign and your ruin, our

victory and your vagrancy, our success and your sorrow.

Satan, delight is for us; depression is for you. Blessing is for us; bitterness is for you. Reward is for us; rejection is for you. Joy is for us; judgment is for you. Transformation is for us; torment is for you. Excitement is for us; ejection is for you. Fortune is for us; failure is for you. Glory is for us; groaning is for you. Immortality is for us; impreachment is for you. A marriage feast is for us; a maddening fright is for you. Peace is for us; persecution is for you. We win and you lose. Go to hell where you belong. We are going to heaven where we belong.

Satan, you can summon all your hosts, but you will lose the battle! For He who is in us is greater than he who is in the world.

We are the Church of the living God—sin washed, Spirit filled, battle scared, unrelenting, and indestructible. The gates of Hell will not prevail against us. So buzz off, you little wimp. You lose; we win, for we have not just grown old; we have continuously grown up toward Christlikeness within the fellowship, friendship, and functions of the Church of our living God.

Satan, we know who is our Commander in Chief. He is Jesus Christ, our resident live-in President. And we will follow Him through thick and thin, through light and darkness, through pleasures and persecutions, through blessings and bitterness, through good and bad, through delights and disasters, through health and sickness, through better and worse, through poverty and riches, through success and failure, through being accepted and rejected, through being loved and hated, through being wanted and excluded, through being heeded and ignored, through being complimented and condemned, through being understood and misunderstood, through being heard and muzzled, and through life and death. Through it all we will stay with our Commander in Chief whom you could not kill and keep down. And you cannot keep us Christians down though you think you might by blitzing us with attractive temptations or by killing us.

Oh no, Satan, that will not happen, because we Christians do not dread the war. We are not here on earth to just plan the war, study the war, evaluate the war or discuss the war. WE CAME TO WIN THE WAR—AND WIN THE WAR WE WILL, for we are the Christian Church of the Almighty God. WE WIN. YOU LOSE!

15

There Never Was Another: Christ Is Worth Representing

Most Christians have no doubt memorized, "For God so loved the world that He gave His only begotten Son . . .(John 3:16, NASB). What kind of Son? The original language translated "only begotten" literally means "one of a kind." The New International Version captures the original word with "one and only." Jesus was the unique One. **There never was another—** and **never will be another** Son exactly like Jesus in every way. How unique is that Son of God?

There never was another who was a human child and also a divine Son; who was the Savior of men, but crucified by men; who was wounded by Satan, yet destroyed Satan; who was man's perfect God, yet God's perfect man.

There never was another who was God's lion, but also God's lamb; who was king of the highest, yet servant of the lowest; who could feed thousands with a lad's lunch, yet hungered Himself.

There never was another who could wipe away all tears, yet wept; who was perfect, but chose imperfect followers; who was sinless, yet bore our sins on the cross; who knew all about God, but who grew up regularly attending the synagogue, and listening to rabbis teach.

There never was another who knew the issues of the scholars, yet taught and spoke to the issues of children; who understood all philosophies and theologies, yet spoke simply and practically; who died, yet reigns forever; who saved others, but would not save Himself.

There never was another who was the Holy One of God, yet still friend of unholy people; who was wisdom incarnate, yet called "mad"; who was the King of glory, but refused every crown except a crown of thorns; who was the Prince of peace, yet was accused as the disturber of peace; who was the Lord of the Sabbath, but was accused as a Sabbath breaker.

There never was another who was truth embodied, but accused of being a liar; who condemned demons, yet was accused of doing the work of demons; who loved all, yet was hated by so many; who owns the world, yet became earthly poor so we might become eternally rich.

There never was another who knew all the wrongs in the Church, but will not abandon her; who had perfect memory, but will forget all the forgiven sins of His people; who became the Son of man, so that we might become the sons and daughters of God; who created the complexities of the cosmic system, but taught with illustrations from common life.

There never was another who was the genius above all, yet was a master of simple words; whose name is above every name, yet is used as a curse word; who blesses so richly, yet is cursed repeatedly; who had power to remove mountains, yet so gentle He would not break a reed.

There never was another who performed so many miracles, but did not use a miracle to keep from being executed; who had so much truth, yet packaged it in so much grace; who had so much power, yet joined it with so much patience; who knows all about us, yet loves us; who had reasons to be so proud, yet so humble; who could control, but submitted; who deserved to be served, yet washed the feet of others; who was the living water, yet thirsted for water to live; who was the creator, yet became a part of the creation.

With the Father and the Holy Spirit, He is the central figure in the Bible. In Genesis—the creator; in Exodus—the Passover; in Leviticus—our high priest; in Numbers—the daily presence in our wildernesses; in Deuteronomy—our manna; in Joshua—the captain of our conquests; in

There Never Was Another: Christ Is Worth Representing

Judges—our deliverer; in Ruth—the one who will lodge with us; in Kings and Chronicles—the servant-King; in Ezra—the fulfillment of God's promise; in Nehemiah—the builder of broken walls; in Esther—the one who came to the kingdom for such a time as this; in Job—the helpful friend; in Psalms—everything from lamb to lion; in Proverbs—our wisdom; in Ecclesiastes—the reason for living; in Song of Solomon—our affirming lover; in Isaiah—the one who sacrificed for us; in Lamentations—the compassionate one; in Ezekiel—the giver of life to dry bones; in Daniel—our companion in the fires of life; in Hosea—the forgiving husband; in Joel—the one who promises the Holy Spirit; in Amos—the helper of the poor; in Obadiah—our vindicator; in Jonah—the bridge across human barriers; in Micah—our hope; in Nahum—the visiting comforter; in Habakkuk—the faithful one; in Zephaniah—the voice of one crying in the wilderness; in Haggai—the restorer of our inheritance; in Zechariah—the son of David; in Malachi—the sovereign one of God.

In Matthew—the Jewish Messiah; in Mark—the servant Messiah; in Luke—the universal Messiah; in John—the divine Messiah; in Acts—the reconciler of all categories of people; in Romans—the justifier; in 1 Corinthians—love; in 2 Corinthians—the forgiver; in Galatians—our liberty; in Ephesians—our unifier; in Philippians—our joy; in Colossians—the image of God; in 1 Thessalonians—the comforter; in 2 Thessalonians—the one who will come again; in 1 Timothy—our mediator; in 2 Timothy—the spirit of power, and love, and self-control; in Titus—the faithful pastor; in Philemon—the trusted friend; in Hebrews—the superior one; in James—the practical one; in 1 Peter—the holy one; in 2 Peter—the patient one; in 1, 2, 3 John—righteousness wrapped in love; in Revelation—the victorious one.

He is the ABC's of all kinds of people in various situations: To the artist, Jesus is the lovely one; to the baker—the living bread; to the carpenter—the solid foundation; to the doctor—the great physician; to the exhorter—the Word of God; to the farmer—the eternal seed; to the geologist—the rock of ages; to the hostess—the helpful guest; to the importer—quality that does not depreciate; to the jeweler—the pearl of great price; to the king—the King of kings; to the locksmith—the key to the kingdom; to the master—the perfect servant; to the newscaster—the good news; to the optometrist—the light of the world; to the philosopher—wisdom; to the questioner—the truthful answer; to the ruler—the Lord of lords; to the scientist—the one who holds all things together; to the theologian—the author of our faith; to the undertaker—the conqueror of death; to the victim—the rescuer; to the x-ray technician—the transparent one; to the warrior—the commander in chief; to the youth—the perfect model; to the zany—laughter that lasts.

No wonder He is called the indescribable gift (2 Corinthians 9:15). At His command demons flee; diseases melt; nature obeys; a sea becomes an Interstate highway; rocks become water; the sun fails to shine; leprosy is cleansed; the lame leap; the earth stops its rotation; the deaf hear; the blind see; the dumb speak; the dead rise to life; leaves on fruit trees wither; water becomes wine; sins are forgiven; stormy winds and waves become calm; fish and loaves multiply; and heaven speaks.

His character will never tarnish. His happiness will never disappear. His hope will never empty. His joy will never decline. His love will never stop. His light will never dim. He holiness will never change. His forgiveness will never empty. His purity will never be defiled. His strength will never weaken. His gentleness will never be rude. His kindness will never become mean. His faithfulness will never falter. His patience will never run out. His goodness will never become bad. His mercy will never neglect. His self-control will never get out-of-control. His energy will never run down. His friendship will never turn against us. His closeness will never become distant. His help will never fail.

For the broken—He mends. For the sinners—He forgives. For the captured—He rescues. For the lost—He looks and finds. For the hurting—He heals. For the lonely—He befriends. For the excluded—He includes. For the hated—He loves. For the separated—He unites. For the addicted—He liberates. For the outsider—He invites. For the workers—He rewards. For the depressed—He counsels. For the grieving—He understands. For the poor—He provides. For the rich—His befriends without a hidden agenda. For the falling—He catches. For the one in the pits—He lifts. For the worker—He rewards. For the generous—He out gives. For the dead—He raises to eternal life.

To sing "There's just something about His name" is far too limited. For there is everything wonderful about His name—His life—His words—His ministry—His salvation—His power—His character—His presence—His love—His death—His resurrection—His ascension—His return to this earth.

There Never Was Another: Christ Is Worth Representing

That same Jesus came not only to us, but also for us. And He invites us to represent Him on earth. To represent is to re-present Him through the way we live. That's why we are to continuously mature into His relational likeness.

And that same Jesus invites us to live forever with Him.

What an offer!

What a grace!

What a love!

What an eternity!

What a Savior!

What a gift!

No wonder the triune God declares to, "The Lord works righteousness and justice for all the oppressed . . . .The lord is compassionate and gracious, slow to anger, abounding in love. He will not always accuse, nor will he harbor his anger forever; he does not treat us as our sins deserve or repay us according to our iniquities. For as high as the heavens are above the earth, so great is his love for those who fear [respect] him; as far as the east is from the west, so far has he removed our transgressions from us. As a father has compassion on his children, so the lord has compassion on those who fear [respect]; for he knows how we are formed . . .(Psalms 103:6-14. Brackets mine).

And," When you pass through the waters, I will be with you. When you pass through the rivers, they will not sweep over you. When you walk through the fire, you will not be burned; the flames will not set you ablaze. For I am the Lord, your God. . ..**Since you are precious and honored in my sight, because I love you.**" (Isaiah 43:2-4. Bold mine).

And, "Forget the former things; do not dwell on the past. See I am doing a new thing! Now it springs up; do you not perceive it? I am making a way in the desert and streams in the desert" (Isaiah 43:18-19).

And, "I, even I, am he who blots out your transgressions, for my own sake, and remembers your sins no more" (Isaiah 43:25.

No wonder, the Psalmist wrote, "This I know that God is for me" (Psalm 56:9). Those eight words sum up the triune God in the Bible from the first verse, "In the beginning God created the heavens and the earth" to the last verse, "The grace of the Lord Jesus be with God's people. Amen" (Genesis 1:1; Revelation 22:21).

Becoming Fully Human In An Inhuman World

The questions for us is this: "Is God pleased with the way He watches you grow up to the potential of being fully human in an inhuman world?"

Several years ago, I saw a plague that a husband designed for his wife with these words, "May you have a thousand reasons to smile today, and may I be just one."

May the triune God have a thousand—no, millions of reasons to smile today, and may you be one of those reasons as you advance toward being conformed to the likeness of Christ becoming fully human in an inhuman world.

Appendix I

Issues To Ponder And Apply From Each Chapter

Chapter 1

1. Brainstorm the relational characteristics (attitudes and actions) the three persons of the Trinity would share with and for each other (such as mutual respect). List on one piece of paper as many as you can.

2. Based on your list from number one above, and given that humans were created in God's image and likeness, and later recreated in that image by being in Christ, create some specific situations between people. Discuss how you should demonstrate specific relational characteristics that you identified with the persons of the Trinity and how that might play out created specific situations. (Example: A person disagrees with the way you interpret a passage of Scripture).

3. Re-read the A-Z expressions of love, and discuss a very specific way to demonstrate each to a very specific situation. Be very specific and practical. (Example: letter M—"to maximize others and not minimize them." Discuss how to do that for a classmate who got an F on a paper, or someone fired from work and is really down in the dumps).

Chapter 2

1. Ponder/discuss the truth that being fully human is to act and react the way God would by demonstrating the characteristics of the Holy Spirit in Galatians 5:22-23; AND being inhuman is to not relate to self, God, others, things, and the devil the way God would.

2. Read the parable of the Good Samaritan (Luke 10). Identify which person is being human and which is being inhuman. Then list the fruit of the Spirit that was or was not applied by each of those persons.

3. Ponder/share specific situations you observed this past week or two that were either human or inhuman, and ponder/discuss why.

4. List a human attitude and a corresponding specific action that relates to a specific situation in a home setting. For instance: a child brought home from school a failing paper. Ponder/discus a human (God-like) attitude (inner feeling), and a specific action (what to say or do) that would be like God's. Make up several situations, real or unreal, to ponder/discuss in which people are more human in their actions and reactions.

5. Now for the same situations in number four, list an inhuman attitude and a corresponding inhuman action.

6. Do number our and five for a public situation, such as someone cutting in line at an amusement park, or someone wanting to change lanes on a crowded freeway.

Appendix I

7. For the following week, keep a list of conducts you notice that are really human actions and a list of those that are inhuman.

8. Make a similar list of your own actions and attitudes that are human and those that are inhuman.

Chapter 3

Discuss number seven above.

1. Brainstorm as many "trees of knowledge of good and evil" you can (non-God sources from which people draw to determine what is right and wrong). Example: types of 111video games.

2. Ponder/discuss why each "tree" listed is attractive to people and the specific results to a culture when that "tree" becomes the regular way people think. Example: video games that give points for killing people. Result—weakens value of another's life that could justify killing, raping, abusing, etc.

3. List and ponder/discuss the "trees" that pull you in. What is there about each tree that allures you? How does that "tree" affect your morality, and relationships to yourself, to God, and to others?

4. This week, look for and list examples of the little "l" kind of life and the Big "L" kind of life. Bring those to the next meeting to discuss.

5. Ponder/discuss any small "l" kinds of things you recently did and the big "L" kinds of things you did. (Doing this helps us to see those two different kinds of life in each of us).

Chapter 4

Discuss number four above.

1. Brainstorm as many privileges you can that we receive or could receive from God.

2. Brainstorm all the categories of people in your geographical area who are not attending your congregation.

3. From number two, ponder/discuss why they are not attending.

4. Ponder/discuss things you do or do not do that help or hinder you being a blessing to ALL kinds, and not to just a few kinds—or just the kind of people who are just like you.

5. Ponder/discuss specific ways you exclude, or simply neglect, or ignore people in the following categories:

    a. Health, i.e. those with Aids.
    b. Gender, i.e. women or men at the work place or in church ministries.
    c. Occupations, i.e. those who are unemployed or in jobs we would not do or want our children to do, but are moral without much social status. List some of those jobs.
    d. Economics, i.e. the very rich or the very poor, including the homeless.
    e. Age, i.e. the senior saints (kind of music and service), and small children (those in the womb, not yet born, and those who are not loved at home).

6. Now return to the above list and ponder/discuss specific ways to include them as Jesus did and would. What can we do personally or organizationally? BE VERY SPECIFIC AND PRACTICAL.

Appendix I

Chapter 5

1. Brainstorm and list the different kinds of people Jesus included in His relationships and ministries.

2. List specific ways you and the church could relate and minister to those same kinds of people in various situations.

3. Read Luke 4:18-19. Ponder/discuss various current day kinds people situations that parallel the situations in this passage among the poor and the prisoners, the blind, and the oppressed. Then ponder/discuss very specific actions the church and individuals, including yourself, could and should do for people in those situations.

4. Ponder/discuss specific ways to help the following feel valued and wanted:

    a. a new person at work.
    b. a visitor to the church.
    c. a new student at the college whose family lives too many miles away for occasional visits.
    d. List other situations and discuss.

5. Make up a different and a very specific situation at home, at the church, and at work for each fruit of the Spirit, and write in how a responsive action that demonstrates that specific fruit in a specific way to that specific situation: example at work: someone got the promotion you thought you would get, what action could you take to demonstrate love—unselfish response—to that person?

Becoming Fully Human In An Inhuman World

	AT HOME	AT CHURCH	AT WORK
LOVE	SITUATION	SITUATION	SITUATION
	ACTION	ACTION	ACTION
JOY	SITUATION	SITUATION	SITUATION
	ACTION	ACTION	ACTION
PEACE	SITUATION	SITUATION	SITUATION
	ACTION	ACTION	ACTION
PATIENCE	SITUATION	SITUATION	SITUATION
	ACTION	ACTION	ACTION

Appendix I

	AT HOME	AT CHURCH	AT WORK
KINDNESS	SITUATION	SITUATION	SITUATION
	ACTION	ACTION	ACTION
GOODNESS	SITUATION	SITUATION	SITUATION
	ACTION	ACTION	ACTION
FAITHFUL	SITUATION	SITUATION	SITUATION
	ACTION	ACTION	ACTION
GENTLE	SITUATION	SITUATION	SITUATION
	ACTION	ACTION	ACTION

Chapter 6

1. Whereas to "sin" is to "miss the mark," review Genesis 1:26 and ponder/discuss what mark is missed when we sin. Then list some sins and show what specific characteristics of God are missed by each one.

2. How does the resurrection of Jesus prove that He had no sin of His own?

3. How does our resurrection prove that our sins were forgiven by Jesus' sacrifice on the cross?

4. Discuss Jesus' death as related to the following aspects:

    a. What caused Jesus to experience the small "d" kind of death?
    b. What caused Jesus to experience the big "D" death?
    c. Why will those in Christ not taste the big "D" death?

5. How does receiving God's *sperma*—seed (1 John 3:9) relate to being born again from above, as Jesus described to Nicodemus in John 3?

6. Name as many things/issues a newborn baby needs during the first few years of its life. Discuss how each of those needs can be met and by whom? Then relate each of those listed needs to a new Christian, and ponder/discuss how each can be met and by whom. Then outline a program the church could develop to properly help mature them into Christlikeness.

Chapter 7

1. Ponder/discuss how you think most people understand Romans 8:28.

Appendix I

2. List specific events in your own personal life and ponder/discuss how each could help you advance toward God's goal mentioned in Romans 8:29.

3. What factors in our culture hinder people from growing up to Christlikeness?

4. What factors in our churches hinder people from growing up to Christlikeness?

5. List at least five events that could happen in a person's life and discuss specific ways you personally could help that person mature into Christlikeness because of each of those events. Ponder/discuss specific ways the local church could help.

6. What specific steps can you take when you become a leader in the church to implement the connection of Romans 8:28 with Romans 8:29? If not a leader?

Chapter 8

1. List some specific reasons new Christians do not mature?

2. List specific functions a literal good shepherd does for his sheep. Ponder/discuss specific ways each of those functions could be done by church leaders and members. Which ones could you do?

3. What could a Christian college and a church do to help people become a shepherd kind of people with newborn "sheep" (new Christian) or a new member?

4. Discuss specific steps that could help apply some of the 52 characteristics of a mature leader mentioned in this chapter. Be specific, such as number 15—"Encourage." Perhaps you could be on the lookout for a visitor to the church who sits alone. Then sit next to that person, strike up a conversation after service, or offer

to take that person to lunch or for a cup of coffee. BE VERY SPECIFIC WITH EACH OF THE 52 CHARACTERISTICS. BRAINSTORM TOGETHER WITH OTHERS IN THE SMALL GROUP FOR PUTTING HANDS AND FEET TO THESE RELATIONAL FIFTY-TWO CHARACTERISTICS.

Chapter 9

1. What are specific things you could do personally to tighten fellowship with others on a campus, at work, in a church, in a family?

2. What are specific things could a church do to tighten fellowship among her members?

3. Ponder/discuss your personal prayer life—when do you usually utter, how long each day, what kinds of prayers you usually utter?

4. Practice each of the different kinds of prayers.

5. With others do the *Lectio Divina* explained in the chapter.

Chapter 10

1. For a week, record how you used your tongue in ways that hurt someone else; and also in ways that helped someone else. Ponder/discuss this. Bring your information next week.

2. List positive and negative tongue habits you have developed, such as complaining, gossiping, putting other people down, encouraging, honoring, etc. Ponder/discuss steps to change the negative habits.

3. What are steps needed to forgive someone, and which are the hardest for you to do?

Appendix I

4. List specific temptations that relate to your own personal weaknesses.

5. Which steps for resisting temptation are hardest for you to do, and why?

6. Write a commitment statement with a specific way to overcome the steps that are hardest for you. Ponder/discuss when you were tempted and the steps you did or cid not take to resist, or did not take.

7. Ask one person to be your accountability partner who will ask you how you are doing in specific situations.

Chapter 11

Discuss the project in number one above.

1. What are specific ways you can be first class mail in the family, at the work place, and in the church?

2. What are your normal reactions to changes in the church you do not like at first? Then review the ABC's of embracing changes, and circle the ones you need to develop. Ponder/discuss those you circled and develop some specific steps to change yourself.

3. Who are the kinds of persons with whom you prefer not to relate? Are there any you know in your environment (in the church, on a college campus, in a family, etc.?) List steps Jesus would take to overcome that resistance. Then list steps you should take.

4. Since eternal life refers to the KIND of life, as well as to the TIME of life, list as many quality aspects of life you think will be normal in heaven. Ponder/discuss ways to apply each of those on earth to fulfill the prayer, "Your will be done on earth as it is done in heaven."

Chapter 12

1. How can the content of this chapter help your teaching and preaching ministry? For instance, when teaching or preaching about anger or faith what kind of content should be included?

2. How can the content of this chapter help you plan worship services? For instance, consider the holistic benefits of tranquility and laughter.

3. What factors in this chapter may have weakened your immunity system in the past or may be negatively affecting your health now?

4. From this and the previous chapters, write a two-page paper titled, "The Purpose of God's Commands." Make copies and share with each member of the small group.

Chapter 13

1. Why do some people think it is impossible to mature to Christlikeness before getting to heaven?

2. Considering God's purpose and mission on earth, why is it important for His newborn children to mature while on earth?

3. What are some essential marks of a mature Christian?

4. Brainstorm as many different ways a person can help self mature.

5. Brainstorm as many different ways we can help others mature.

6. Brainstorm as many different programs a church can develop to help people mature.

7. What are areas a church could assess in order to measure its own spiritual and relational maturity?

8. What are areas you can assess about your own personal life to measure your own spiritual and relational maturity?

Chapter 14

1. What are the "attractions" that come your way that distract you from being Jesus' special friend through life?

2. What are the disciplines you have practiced to mature spiritually and relationally?

3. What are the disciplines you have not practiced?

4. What are the disciplines you have been taught , but have not taught others?

5. List all the ways you have spiritually and relationally changed during the course of studying this book.

6. List the ways you want to change over the next two years. For each item listed, write specific steps needed to change with a date for starting each step.

Chapter 15

Each day for as long as it takes review each description of Jesus in the order presented and meditate upon that description. Visualize Jesus demonstrating that description. Then meditate how you can personally demonstrate in a specific way Jesus' humanity.

Appendix II

An Eleven-Week Program Engaging Spiritual Disciplines

Week 1

THE DISCIPLINE OF SOLITUDE AND SILENCE

Solitude and Silence

Silence and solitude are two of the deepest and most difficult disciplines for some people to experience. That is because we have become addicted to activities and noise.

Silence and solitude go together like a saddle and a horse. Together they quiet the spirit, soul, and, body.

Appendix II

Solitude

Jesus often practiced the discipline of solitude. He got away by Himself between the times of His baptism and public ministry (forty days in the wilderness), at the end of a busy day of activities, after hearing the execution of John the Baptist, before making significant decisions, and during the height of His ministry when He was in great demand. If Jesus recognized He needed times for solitude, shouldn't we?

How to Engage in Solitude

1. Get away from people, animals, activities, and noise to be alone.
2. Choose a location and a time of day.
3. Disconnect the cell phone.
4. Sit in silence.
5. Close your eyes.
6. Empty the mind of planned thoughts.
7. Keep the mind open to be better able to encounter God's presence in quietness.
8. Eliminate ungodly thoughts that enter the mind.

Silence

Many times God's communications are drowned out by noise and chatter. There is a time to be silent and a time to speak (Ecclesiastes 3:7). Silence requires that you not verbally talk.

Benefits of Silence

1. Helps us listen—a listening silence.
2. Slows us down—hushes the rushes.
3. Clears interruptions to make room for inward attentiveness.
4. Allows a person to view one's own motives, strengths, and weaknesses.

5. Helps a person experience the presence of God.
6. Helps the person be more creative with thoughts, ideas, and plans.
7. Helps liberate the person from having quick answers and fixes to the needs of self and others.
8. Helps a person let go of frustrations and anger.
9. Quiets the spirit, soul, and body.
10. Helps a person develop inner contentment and peace.
11. Helps liberate a person from being addicted to speaking.
12. Centers the total self on God's presence.

Steps for Developing the Discipline of Silence

1. Develop natural quiet times, such as, right after getting up; waiting times; muting out commercials on television; turning off the radio and television; disconnecting the phone; walking; exercising; showering; and so on.
2. Select a private place and a time for silence each day, and visit it.
3. Practice being quick to hear and slow to speak.
4. Spend an entire day without saying a word and journal your experience.
5. Go on a silent two-day retreat every year or two in order to disconnect from so much rushing, activities. While on the retreat, you can do such things as reading, silently praying, reflecting, writing, walking, meditating, planning, and so on.
6. Begin contributing fewer words without less input in a meeting.

Experiencing Silence

1. Begin by spending five consecutive minutes in silence.
2. Gradually increase the time until you are able to be silent for at least 30 minutes.

Week 2

THE DISCIPLINE OF MEDITATION

What is it?

1. Inner listening to feelings and body language.
2. Inner rehearsing, reviewing, ruminating, and contemplating pleasures, positive situations, and sights.
3. Inner centering the mind on one thing, and staying attentive to it.
4. Inner visualizing something in the mind that the eye does not see.
5. Inner imagining. This is not something new. For instance, when a person tells a scary story, our heart rate increases and blood pressure rises as we imagine the scenes. When we imagine a calming scene, the body relaxes. Medical research has documented the remission of some cancer when patients imagined the destruction of some cancer cells.
6. Inner speaking. This is a way for the mind and body to speak to each other and in doing so the mind and body affect each other.
7. Inner awareness of and attentiveness to the presence of God.
8. This is not Eastern mysticism that transfers the inner self into a state of nothingness.

What it does

1. Provides a process for fulfilling 2 Corinthians 4:16-18, "Therefore we do not lose heart. Though outwardly we are wasting away, yet inwardly we are being renewed day by day. . .So we fix our eyes not on what is seen, but on what is unseen. . .."
2. Provides a process for fulfilling Colossians 3:1-2, "Since, then, you have been raised with Christ, set your hearts on things above, where Christ is seated at the right hand of God. Set your minds on things above, not on earthly things."

3. Provides a process for fulfilling Romans 12:2, "Do conform any longer to the pattern of this world, but be transformed by the renewing of your mind."
4. Provides a process for redirecting our thoughts that can help redirect our lives.
5. Provides a process for feeling "at home" with God.
6. Provides a process for inner surrendering that can help change the lifestyle to God's.

Topics for Focused Meditation

1. On God's Word.
2. On God's promises.
3. On God's character.
4. On God's works.
5. On God's holistic personhood—the Father, Son, and Holy Spirit.
6. On God's creation.
7. On scenes of Jesus' ministry.
8. On scenes of Jesus' execution.
9. On expected scenes of Jesus' return.
10. On the fruit of the Spirit.
11. On heaven.
12. On a specific biblical text.
13. On God's will for current situations.
14. On the positive aspects of self, others, and experiences (Philippians 4:8-10).
15. On diseases in your body—meditate healing.

An Alternative Meditative Practice

1. Sit in a chair with feet on the floor and hands on the lap with palms up.
2. Close the eyes.
3. Relax the muscles from top to bottom.
4. Breathe in and out slowly.

5. Visualize a peaceful scene, such as a garden, a calm ocean, a peaceful valley, sitting at Jesus' feet, a positive and compassionate activity of Jesus, a sleeping baby, and so on.
6. Select a word or short phrase, such as "God loves me; I am precious to God; I am God's child; Jesus loves me; God is good; God is gracious; Jesus is my friend", and so on.
7. Repeat the word or phrase over and over silently while visualizing the same peaceful scene.
8. Do this for at least ten minutes.
9. Then sing or whisper a song.
10. Keep a journal of your feelings following each meditation period.

Week 3

BREATH PRAYERS

PRAYER INFORMATION

We Tap into The Heart of God

Community is a word that describes a state of commUNITY=Community. Communication is one essential process for reaching a state of community. We will not enjoy community with anyone with whom we will not communicate.

Prayer is one form of community with God that refines and tightens our closeness to Him. Prayer helps narrow any gap we might have widened between self and God, and between self and others.

The reasons Christians have immediate and personal availability to God but not to the President of the United States are many:

1. God knows each person's name, character, activities, strengths, weaknesses, joys, sorrows, perplexities, and so on.

2. We have affirmed and accepted His love and grace that He extended through His Son, Jesus.
3. We are His children in Christ.
4. God has already declared, "You are honored and precious in my sight, because I love you" (Isaiah 43:4).
5. God has already promised that He is close to the brokenhearted (Psalm 34:18).
6. God has compassion for us (Psalms 103:13).

God Taps into Our Prayers

1. The Father listens.
2. The Son listens.
3. The Holy Spirit listens.

God Responds to Our Prayers

Because our needs are different, His answers are diverse that include the following:

1. No! And His "no" comes from His "know." He knows His plans, and what is best for us.
2. Slow! Not now, but later. So don't stop asking.
3. Go! Yes, this will happen.

What prayer is not

1. A mini-sermon. Don't preach for others to hear.
2. Theological special verbiage. Use everyday words.

Appendix II

What Prayer Is

1. Chatting with God.
2. Speaking with Him from the heart and from the lips.
3. Co-partnering with God.
4. Being transparent.
5. Recognizing the finite (limited) one is coming into contact with the infinite (unlimited) One.

Reasons Some May Give For Not Praying

1. "I'm not sure what to say or how to say it." We can talk with God as we talk with another person. After all, He is our Abba—our Daddy (Romans 8:15; Galatians 4:6). Nothing—no-thing—is too small or too big to share with Him.
2. "I'm not sure I have enough faith." All of God's leaders in the Bible had faith mixed with doubt. But God looks through doubts to see whatever little seed of faith there is. He will latch on to that and work with us. For instance, when Peter started walking on water he demonstrated big faith, but then demonstrated little faith when he began to sink. But Jesus latched on to what He described as Peter's "little faith", and did not allow him to drown. Through the prophet, God told King Hezekiah that he would die. Hezekiah had enough faith to believe it and prayed. God sent the prophet back to tell Hezekiah that He heard his prayer, saw his tears, would heal him, and give him 15 more years. Hezekiah believed the bad news, but doubted the good news; however, God looked beyond Hezekiah's lack of faith in the good news and latched on to whatever faith he had and healed him (2 Kings 20:1-11).

Diversity of Prayers

The Psalms is a collection of more than one person's prayer journal, many of which were put to music and became one of Israel's hymnbooks. In that journal are prayers of requesting, interceding, bragging, confessing, questioning, complaining, remembering, wondering, repenting, revenging, instructing, doing small talk, love talk, and so on. This diversity reveals that nothing embarrasses God, who is big enough to listen to anything we share even if some of it comes across as ungodly and ugly.

That we can share with God anything that is on our mind is no better demonstrated than in Psalm 44:23, "Wake up Lord. Why are you sleeping when I have a need?" (My translation.)

Introducing the Discipline of Breath Prayers

These are short simple prayers (chats) that are spoken in one breath throughout the day as a person experiences both simple and complex realities. Through its brevity, a person senses the nearness of God and intimacy with God. A person shares simple things with God that he/she would likely share with a human companion. Some examples:

- "I just now goofed."
- "I wish this traffic would speed up."
- "What a beautiful full moon that is."
- "Come along and walk with me my friend, God."
- "Help me to hold my tongue right now."
- "Father, give some joy to—(name a person."
- "Father, forgive me for thinking like that."
- "Wow! I really feel good right now."
- "I feel rotten right now."

Engaging the Discipline of Breath Praying

1. Practice breath prayers throughout each day.
2. Notice the closeness with God as you share your thoughts about big and little encounters, and with various kinds of responses.
3. Carry a little notebook and write down each breath prayer for at least a week.
4. Record your experience in a Prayer Journal.

Appendix II

Week 4

THE DISCIPLINE OF THE PRAYER OF REQUESTING

PRAYER INFORMATION

Taking Time to Pray

In the Garden of Gethsemane, Jesus asked His apostles, "Could you not watch with me [pray] one hour?" And they did not know what to say to Him (Mark 14:40). When we get to heaven, would we know what to say should God address us with, "Not once did you ever spend one hour on any day talking with me. Was I not that important to you? Why could you not have spent one hour on any day talking with me before you got here?"

How would we answer that in light of the many other things we will have spent an hour a day doing, such as getting ready to go somewhere, talking to others, working, driving, waiting in lines at an amusement park or in a doctor's office, reading, playing, taking walks, doing other exercises, eating, doing a hobby, watching television, talking on the telephone, watching a movie, using the Internet, and so on?

We could easily spend an hour a day talking with God/Jesus if we planned for it. One way might be to use dead times, which are periods we could be talking with God while doing something else, such as waiting, driving, riding, walking, doing chores, getting ready to go somewhere, muting out commercials on television, turning off television, and so on. These are good times to schedule God into our conversations. After all, don't we talk to others during these times?

Another way we could spend an hour a day in prayer is to pray the entire the Lord's Prayer either at the same time or pray a selected phrase at different times.

Jesus' apostles saw Jesus do unbelievable miracles, but never once was it recorded that they requested, "Teach us to do miracles like that." They watched Him teach in ways that thousands came to hear, but they never once asked, "Teach us to teach like that." They listened to Him take difficult questions and answer them with one or two sentences, but never approached Him with, "Teach us to deal with questions like that." But these grown men, who were used to praying three times a day, heard Jesus talking to God, and one day came to Jesus with, "Teach us to pray" (Luke 11:1). Jesus replied, "Pray in this manner" (meaning, "like this"). He then taught them what we call the Lord's Prayer. Actually this is the Disciples' Prayer or the Students' Prayer (for that's what disciples are) or the Seeker's Prayer, or the New Christian's Prayer. Although it is brief, it is a wonderful and effective prayer for developing longer prayer times with God.

Matthew 5:9-13 records the longer version of this Students' Prayer. It is not difficult to spend an hour a day praying through this prayer. Over the next several weeks we will work with a different phrase or word of this prayer, along with a different kind of prayer.

The First Phrase of the Lord's Prayer

"Our Father." When praying this phrase, first focus on just the word, "Father." Now think about what it means to have a good father or parent. Be specific. Each day this week talk with God about one good father kind of characteristic and function, and brag about that to God. That could include such things as the fact that He birthed you through Christ even though He knew what He was going to get with you before you were born, but He did not abort you; knows how you have messed up, but He never abused you; knows all about you, but never tattles; He had a broken heart when you really disappointed Him, but traded Jesus on the cross for you; He is proud of you when you do something good or well; brags to the angels about you; He is willing to be inconvenienced for you; and so on. Then commit to specific situations in which you can demonstrate those characteristics to others. Select very specific situations with names, times, and places.

Next, focus on "Our." "You are not just MY Father, but are OUR Father." Thank Him for connecting you to others in His local and global family. Talk about Jesus being your brother who models the Father for you, (Hebrews 2:11). Pick up on the fact that you are a co-heir with Jesus and will inherit what God owns (Romans 8:15-17; Galatians 4:1-7; 1

Appendix II

Peter 1:3-5). Ask the Father to help you treat His other kids, your brothers and sisters in Christ, as God wants His other kids treated. Deal with how you are treating some of them by name, and be specific about talking to the Father about helping you to be a better brother or sister to all of God's other kids. Recognize His kids who are different from you, and who are members in different church fellowships.

Reasons Some May Give for Not Praying

1. "God already knows my needs." But that is a reason to talk with Him about them. It is one thing for me to know something about my grown children's needs, but they usually view it as interfering when I fill a need without their desire that I do it. But when they ask, I am thrilled to be included, and it does my heart good to help. It is one thing for God to know you have a need, but it is another thing for you to let Him know that you want Him to know. That brings Him into the need with your desire, love, and trust. In Isaiah 65, God declared that He was available, "I am here. I am here." He was ready to answer their requests, but they did not ask. Our Father in heaven will not force Himself as an intruder on you.

2. "I already asked once." When you were little children did you ask your parents only once for something you really wanted? To keep asking is to affirm that you value whatever it is that you request. God honors persistent asking. If you doubt that, read the parable in Luke 18:1-8 that begins with "Then Jesus told his disciples a parable **to show them that they should always pray and not give up** (Bold print mine). I suspect Jesus' parables came from actual events. I doubt that He made up an untrue story to illustrate an eternal truth. Jesus concluded the Luke 18 parable with, "when the Son of Man comes, will he find faith on the earth?" In that context, faith was tied to a person who repeatedly asks. To ask only once could communicate that you don't value the request, don't believe God is able to do what you ask, does not love you enough to do so, or you have already decided He will not answer it. Also read Matthew 15:21-28. To the woman kept asking, Jesus

said, "Woman, you have great faith" (28). Jesus used the present tense verb when He said to ask, seek, and knock, which is better translated as "keep on asking, seeking, and knocking" (Matthew 6:7-8).

The Prayer of Requesting

Most of us are good at making requests in our prayers, but are we really THAT good? Here are some guidelines for sharing requests with God:

1. Be very specific. Many times our prayers are too general, such as, "Heal all the sick people," or "Bless the missionaries." If you or another person has a need, be specific with the details of the request. If it is for healing, ask God to intervene into the exact part of the body that is diseased or damaged. If it is for reconciliation with a broken relationship, ask God for help in a very specific aspect, such as to hold your tongue, or help clarify a misunderstanding, which you state in the request. If the request is for finances, state the amount needed, and when needed.
2. Be more inclusive by specifically stating:
   - What happened or did not happen that created this need.
   - How meeting this request will benefit you.
   - How meeting this request will benefit others
   - How meeting this request will benefit God's purpose.
3. Include the will, wishes/desires of God. Chat with God about what you know He wants to do on earth that could be served by fulfilling your request. What would you do with the answer?
4. Invite one or two others to join you in this request. Of course, we would not do that for every request; so choose those for which you want to include others in a concert of prayers. However, do not think that when two or three ask, it WILL AUTOMATICALLY be done. Oh, no! The Greek verb tense is that it WILL HAVE ALREADY BEEN DONE in heaven (Matthew 18:19-20). That means we should be requesting kinds of things **with the kinds of reasons** that agree with the characteristics, conduct, concerns, and content of heaven as

Appendix II

revealed in God's Word and demonstrated by Jesus—a WWJD—"What Would Jesus Do?" and WWJB, "What Would Jesus Be?" and WWJA, "What Would Jesus Ask?"

Engaging the Discipline of the Prayer of Requesting

1. Each day this week include a prayer of request to God in specific terms. It would be good if the same request were made each day (for continuation) that included one of the different guidelines above, until all are used together for the same request.
2. Pray daily the first phrase of the Lord's Prayer.
3. Keep a journal with the dates you made the requests with space to record when and how they were answered.
4. Be patient and consistent. Some people have prayed for years the same specific request before experiencing God's answer.

Week 5

THE DISCIPLINE OF THE PRAYER FOR REMEMBERING AND CONTEMPLATING

PRAYER INFORMATION

A Reason Some May Give For Not Praying

"I don't think I am good enough to pray." Many people think they have to reach a certain level of "goodness" before God will answer prayers. But all of us blow it; we have all fallen short of the character of God (Romans 3:23). To think we are not good enough could come from an attitude of inferiority, or it could come from the attitude of humility.

God listens to us in spite of our faults, and if we are honest, because of our faults. Read Luke 18:9-14, and notice which person was justified.

"Elijah was a man just like us." Did you catch it—a person **just like us?** And his prayers had powerful results. Just because he prayed, it did not rain for 3½ years, and it did not start raining again until he prayed for it. Wow! And that came from a person **just like us** (James 5:17-18).

Don't let your failures silence your feelings toward God's listening ears. Don't let your miseries miss His mercy. We may not be good enough, but God is. And He is good for us (Psalm 56:9).

The Relational Aspects of the Lord's Prayer

Below is one way to see how relational the Lord's Prayer is:

Relating	Father
Including	Our
Positioning	Who is in heaven
Respecting	Hallowed be your name
Outreaching	Your kingdom come
Yielding	Your will be done
Representing	As it is in heaven
Depending	Give us today our daily bread
Confessing	Forgive us our debts (sins)
Forgiving	as we forgive our debtors (those who sin against us)
Following	Lead us not
Resisting	Into temptation
Trusting	But deliver us
Recognizing	From evil
Honoring	Yours is
God's authority	The kingdom
His ability	The power
His character	The glory
His eternality	forever

Appendix II

The Second Phrase of the Lord's Prayer

"Our Father **who is in heaven**" (Bold print mine). Take time to affirm God's position. Let your mind see Him in heaven, and chat with him about what you visualize. This could include something like this, "Father God, no one has knocked you off the throne or ever will. You are not only the Creator of this planet and all planets, but you are also the One who owns it all. Thank you for letting me enjoy some of it. I thank you that you are not trapped to this earthly environment, and you don't cave in to its pressures as we do. In heaven, you see things from a different vantage point than we do. Help others and me to see people, issues, problems, and solutions through your eyes and with your heart. Keep me from being attached to the media, to the music, to the movies, to the monies, and to the mess down here that are so alluring. And thank you for wanting me to be there with you and for continuing to prepare a place for me, so where you are I will be someday

The Prayer of Remembering and Contemplating

This prayer involves the following activities:

1. Remember at least one activity of God, of Jesus, or of the Holy Spirit that is recorded in the Bible or that you have personally experienced.
2. State that activity in detail to God with the attitude of thanksgiving and praise.
3. Contemplate the difference that activity can make if you do it for others.
4. Make a commitment to God about that activity. It might be a commitment to never personally doubt the reality of that activity; to teach others about that activity and the relevance of it for living today; to apply the relevance of that activity through your personal life to others.

NOTE: During the time of Jesus, to remember did NOT mean to merely recall the facts, but also to re-enact or to re-live the significance of the events or person in specific ways. It was to bring something from the past to the present by applying it in very specific ways. THAT IS WHAT WE ARE TO DO THROUGH THE PRAYER OF REMEMBRANCE AND CONTEMPLATION.

The Spirituality of Remembering and Contemplating

The issues of our culture can crowd out remembering just who God is and what He has done. That happened to God's people in past times and it happens today. For instance, read Judges 2:10; 3:7 and Isaiah 1:2-4; 17:10. Peter wrote about the necessity of remembering (2 Peter 1:12-15).

Forgetfulness leads to neglectfulness. Neglectfulness leads to disobedience. Disobedience blocks spiritual development into Christlikeness. We are commanded to not forget. For instance, see Deuteronomy 4:9; 6:12. A good project would be to look up every passage with the words forget and remember to see the essentiality of this for Christians.

We can help fellow Christians catch the significance of the past as they listen to our prayers of remembering and contemplating.

Engaging the Discipline of the Prayer of Remembering and Contemplating

1. Set aside a time each day this week to pray the second phrase of the Lord's Prayer.
2. Set aside a time to utter a prayer of remembering and contemplation.
3. Record these and your experiences in a Prayer Journal.

Week 6

THE DISCIPLINE OF THE PRAYER OF PRAISE

PRAYER INFORMATION

A Reason Some May Use for Not Praying

"The only reason to pray is to change me. Prayer never changes God, so what's the use?"

Changing self is an important reason for praying, but that is not the only benefit. Perhaps one reason some do not think prayer makes a difference is because they may not believe God does supernatural things today as He did in biblical days. Perhaps another reason is that some may believe God is not capable of changing His mind about anything.

The God of the Bible is big enough to listen to our prayers, and because we prayed may change His mind. He did that several times. For instance, His people had made a golden calf, worshipped it, and declared that it was the god that brought them out of Egypt. That ticked off God, who demanded that Moses leave Him alone so He might destroy those people. But Moses begged God not to do that, and kept up those begging prayers for forty days and forty nights. Then God relented (changed His mind) "and did not bring on his people the disaster he had threatened" (Exodus 32:9-14; Deuteronomy 9:18). On another occasion, God decided to destroy His people in order to give Moses a greater nation with whom to work. But Moses asked God not to do that, and God replied, "I have forgiven them, **as you asked**" (Numbers 14:10-20. Bold print mine). God will never change His character nor His mission. But He can, did, and will change His methods, as any excellent Commander-in-Chief would do.

We should not diminish the reality of Psalm 115:3, "Our God is in heaven; **he does whatever pleases Him**" (See also Psalm 135:6; Daniel 4:35. Bold print mine). It pleases Him to listen to our prayers, to respect us, and to change His mind, which lets us know we are important to

Him, and we can make a difference through prayers. Paul affirmed this when he wrote the Corinthians about being delivered from potential death and requested they pray for him, "He has delivered us from such a deadly peril, and he will deliver us. On him we have set our hope that he will continue to deliver us, **as you help us by your prayers.** Then many will give thanks on our behalf for the gracious favor granted us in answer to the prayers of many" (2 Corinthians 1:10-11. Bold print mine).

The Third Phrase of the Lord's Prayer

"Our Father who is in heaven **hallowed be your name.**" In biblical days to use the word "name" was a way to say "person." Thus to be baptized in the "name" of the Father, Son, and Holy Spirit is to be baptized into the "person" of the Father, Son, and Holy Spirit. To pray in the "name" of Jesus is to pray in the "person" of Jesus, that is, to pray as a Christian connected to Him as one who is "in Christ (the most common way in the New Testament to describe a Christian).

"Hallowed" meant to respect. So to pray, "hallowed be your name" is to say, "May You, just as You are, be respected."

When you pray this phrase, you should mention along with it at least one characteristic of God, give Him recognition for being consistent with that characteristic. Share how you personally experienced that characteristic; and ask Him to help that characteristic to mature in you, so you can demonstrate it in very specific ways to very specific persons or situations in order to be God's effective representative on earth.

The Prayer of Praise

Psalms and the book of Revelation are saturated with this kind of prayer. Adoration is our human response to the love, grace, mercy, sacrifice, and service of God to and for us. It affirms what He has done, is doing, and will do. Adoration gives Him verbal credit for being the kind of God He is. Adoration is love talk, such as I love you, I adore you, I cherish you, I desire you, I honor you, and I respect you, I relish you, I treasure you, I value you, I prioritize you, I put nothing between you and me, I affirm you, and so on. This prayer brags about God to God. This prayer offers God the "sacrifice of praise" (Hebrews 13:15). God has a soft and sensitive heart and is touched when we bless Him with praises.

Steps for Praying a Prayer of Praise

1. Think about some of the ways He has served you.
2. Think about some of the wonderful characteristics of God.
3. Read through a few Psalms of praise and adoration.
4. Pray some of these Psalms.
5. Visualize standing before God in heaven with your love talk.
6. Share words that invite Him to clearly look into your heart to see how much you cherish Him.
7. Conclude this prayer with a praise song, such as, "How Great Thou Art"; "God Is So Good"; "Majesty"; "Holy, Holy, Holy", and so on.

Engaging in Prayers of Praise

1. Set aside time every day between today and the next meeting to pray the third phrase of the Lord's Prayer.
2. Set aside time each day to utter love talk with the Father.
3. Set aside time each day to utter love talk with Jesus
4. Set aside time each day to utter love talk with the Holy Spirit. All three are all worthy of being admired. So let them know it by your talk with and to them.
5. Record some of your love talk in a Prayer Journal.

Week 7

THE DISCIPLINE OF THE PRAYER OF YIELDING OR RELINQUISHING

PRAYER INFORMATION

A Reason Some May Use for Not Praying

"I got a 'No' answer for something I really wanted, so I decided not to waste time praying."

God's "No" answers come from God's "Know" position. For instance, I fell in love a few times during my high school days. Each time I prayed that God would see this love through to a marriage. After I attended our first class reunion—the 35th one—and saw those for whom I made that prayer, I quickly thanked God for His "No" answer, and I suspect they did also. An excellent example of God's "No" from His "Know" answer happened to the beloved minister, Wayne Smith. A few years ago, Wayne failed a treadmill test, and was scheduled for an angiogram. During that procedure fifty members from the church met in the hospital's chapel to engage in a concert of prayer asking God to arrange for the problem to be served with medicine without intervention. But God's answer was "No." During the quadruple open-heart bypass surgery, doctors found something that would not have been discovered without that surgery –a hole through the pericardium sac, which completely envelops the heart. Without repairing it, Wayne would have died within a few months from that problem alone. While recuperating at home, Wayne experienced severe pain from a staph infection and was taken back to the hospital. While hospitalized this time he passed blood, which resulted in an exploratory surgery. That surgery discovered a malignant cancer, which would have killed him in a few months. God's "No" to those fifty people praying came from God's "Know" information. We need to be grateful that one of God's answers is a clear, "No," even if the reason may not be as obvious as was this experience for Wayne.

Appendix II

The Fourth Phrase in the Lord's Prayer

"Our Father who is in heaven, hallowed be your name, **your kingdom come, your will be done on earth as it is in heaven**" (Bold print mind). "Your will be done" is paralleled and synonymous with "your kingdom come." God's kingdom refers to His will—His desires/wishes.

This is the time to ask God to intervene and affect situations on earth, so life on earth can better reflect life in heaven. Here are some helpful steps for doing that:

1. List various situations, such as the following:
   A. Your schedule of anticipated situations and events for the day.
   B. Specific situations your family members are experiencing.
   C. Specific situations you know your church is facing.
   D. Specific situations you know missionaries are facing.
   E. Specific situations in the world, such as people starving in a particular country, pornography in the media and on the Internet, drug manufacturers, dealers, and users, the homeless, people having health problems without insurance, civil wars in countries, the increase of AIDS world-wide, and so on.
2. Choose a different specific situation for each day of the week. Or, you might have 30, one for each day of the month
3. Pray about those situations in very specific ways that you know are in tune with God's will, such as, "God, inspire the national leaders to outlaw pornography on the Internet."
4. Be open to the reality that God's will in these situations is usually fulfilled through people.
5. Be open to the fact that God may motivate you to be involved in some way in the answer.

The Discipline of the Prayer of Yielding or Relinquishing

The prayer of yielding or relinquishing is the prayer of letting go, such as in the following situations:

1. Letting go of having to be in control of others.
2. Letting go of trying to be the "fix-it" person.
3. Letting go of always having decisions and situations go your way and in your time.
4. Letting go of attitudes and reactions that are not the Holy Spirit's.
5. Letting go of good things in order to be open to receive better things from God.

Jesus prayed this kind of prayer in the Garden, when He prayed, "Not my will." Here He relinquished His personal will, preference, and desire. In a sense, He crucified His will before going to the cross. To pray this prayer is to yield our will, wishes and desires to God's with, "Thy will be done."

We are to pray this prayer with hope—the hope that God will do His work to transform our will, our ways, our attitudes, our actions, our reactions and even our plans, so we can better be His representatives on earth.

The prayer of yielding is a difficult one. It requires that we be totally transparent, and accept God taking what we yield to Him and doing with it whatever He pleases. That might mean giving it back to us, as He did for Abraham who relinquished His son Isaac to God; and as He did to Jesus, who died on the cross, only to receive it back. But it may also mean that He wants what we relinquish to never be picked up again by us.

This is the one of the most personal prayers you will do. Only you can decide what you need to yield to God. Below are some possibilities that might slip through the cracks:

1. Your ego that gives you a "big head" rather than a "big heart."
2. Your demanding self.
3. Your superiority or inferior complex.
4. Your negative, critical, and pessimistic outlook.
5. Your tendency to procrastinate.
6. Your poor stewardship of finances, time, and talents.
7. Your tendency to worry too much.
8. Your lack of compassion.

Appendix II

9. Your decision to keep that fruit of the Spirit from growing in you and flowing from you.
10. Your closed mind to fresh ideas, concepts, practices, and understandings.
11. Your tongue that gossips and slanders.
12. Your decisions to not keep secrets when shared with you.

Steps for Engaging the Prayer of Yielding

1. Recognize the gap between your will and God's.
2. Empty self of too much self.
3. Surrender your will to God's.
4. Abandon what you know keeps you from being close to God.
5. Release what you yield.
6. Receive what God provides or returns.

Engaging the Prayer of Yielding

1. Set aside time each day to pray the fourth phrase of the Lord's Prayer.
2. Set aside a time each day to pray the yielding prayer.
3. Record what you yielded in a Prayer Journal.

Week 8

THE DISCIPLINE OF THE PRAYER OF CONFESSION

PRAYER INFORMATION

A Reason Some May Use for Not Praying

"Because God has so much on His plate and He knows so many people, He would not be the least bit interested in hearing anything I have to say."

That is an understandable idea, but it fails to understand the Christian's connection to God and God's interest in His kids. He is the Christian's father and has put His own spiritual DNA in us via His *sperma*—His seed (1 John 3:9). Until I became a father I did not understood why God prioritizes us the way He does. When I returned home from a speaking trip, it thrilled me when my small children would run up to me, hug me, and start talking to me. I was all heart and ears for the little things they had to say. I have the same emotions with my grandchildren when they come running into the house with, "Hi Grandpa!" It's not the same when they say, "Hi everyone!" Oh no! It's the "Grandpa" that does it.

When one of my grown kids calls home for no other reason than just to talk, that lifts me to cloud nine. I am very honored when one calls to get some advice. That shows a connection of love, respect, and trust.

And so it is with God, our Father. He is all heart and ears to whatever we have to say. He is touched by our love, respect, and trust. He is not only our Father, but also our Father-friend, which He revealed when He put on human skin in Jesus who was known as a friend of sinners. Friends want to hear from one another, which is one way to nurture a friendship.

Prayer is one of the few things we do on earth that we will continue to do in heaven. Wouldn't it be embarrassing to know that our voice addressing God in heaven sounded strange to Him, because He seldom heard us address Him on earth?

Appendix II

The Fifth Phrase of the Lord's Prayer

"Our Father who is in heaven, hallowed be your name, your kingdom come, your will be done on earth as it is in heaven. **Give us today our daily bread**" (Bold print mine). Notice this prayer is not for wants, dreams, and wishes. When Jesus shared this prayer, bread was an essential need for staying alive, as it is in many parts of the world today. This prayer calls for us to be very specific about our essential needs. These could be needs for having and keeping a job, for having and keeping friends, for having and keeping health, and so on.

This calls for us to intercede for others. Praying this prayers is easier to do if we keep a notebook of our needs and the needs of others including needs of an institution, such as the church, a Christian college, a business, and so on. When it comes to people needs, don't forget the hungry, lonely, excluded, homeless, unemployed, sick, grieving, and so on. Be very specific with names and needs. But notice this prayer is not for MY needs only, but also for OUR needs.

The Discipline of the Prayer of Confession

Confessing to God is one step to receive His forgiveness. The word "confess" in the Greek language literally means to "speak like." That is, to speak with our lips like we believe in our heart. It means to be transparent without pretending to be what we are not. Confessing sin means to give it to God. Don't try to sugar coat it. Give Him the details. Of course, He already knows, but He is pleased when we take steps to show Him we want Him to know. Share it with Him with the belief that He will accept it, honor us for confessing, blot the sin out of His memory, and cleanse us from it, for He promised, "the sins I forgive I will remember no more" (Hebrews 8:12; 10:17. See also 1 John 1:9). Here are some facts of comfort and security when we confess to God:

1. He is eager to accept our confession.
2. He is not angry when we confess.

3. He will not remember forgiven sins.
4. He will not tattle tale on us.
5. He wants to give us forgiveness.
6. He promises to forgive when we confess.
7. He is the original and consistent Promise Keeper.

Characteristics in the Prayer of Confession

1. Examine your inner and outer life, recognize your sin, and take responsibility for it.
2. Do not blame others as Adam and Eve did.
3. Confess to God in humility, because of the sorrow you piled on Him and others.
4. Connect sorrow to humility, not because you were caught or others found out, but because you know that your sins hurt God and the person against whom you sinned.
5. Let sorrow lead you to repentance. The Greek word for repentance literally means to change the mind. Authentic repentance always changes the mind in a way that changes the manners, changes attitudes in a way that changes actions, and it changes perspectives in a way that changes practices.
6. Confess with the determination to avoid repeating the confessed sin.
7. Let your confession clear your mind of that sin and get on with living for God and for others as God's representative.

Engaging the Prayer of Confession

1. Set aside time every day between today and the next meeting to pray the fifth phrase of the Lord's Prayer and the prayer of confession.
2. Record your confession in a Prayer Journal.

Appendix II

Week 9

THE DISCIPLINE OF THE PRAYER OF HEALING

PRAYER INFORMATION

A Reason Some May Use for Not Praying

"Why pray about healing, because God stopped doing miracles after the Bible was completed. So we are just wasting our time asking for a miracle if it would take one for healing."

There is not a single hint in the Bible that suggests God locked up His power after the Bible was completed. This kind of thinking came out of the Age of Enlightenment during which it was taught that there is no influence outside or beyond our universe that can affect anything that happens on this planet, that is the closed system approach, which denied the reality of miracles.

God has always been able to do what is impossible from the human perspective. Missionaries have seen many miracles, but many are reluctant to share them for fear a church that has de-powered God would cut off funds if those missionaries really believe God is still doing miracles.

Early in Abraham's life God asked, "Is anything too hard for the Lord?" Then He proved that nothing was (Genesis 18:14). Later, God challenged His people's disbelief with, "Was my arm too short. . .Do I lack the strength. . .?"(Isaiah 50:2). The angel declared an eternal truth to Mary, "For nothing is impossible with God" (Luke 1:37). Jesus declared, "With man this is impossible, but with God all things are possible" (Matthew 19:26). The God who could stop the rotation of the earth without getting anything out of balance except the length of the day; who could open the sea for three million people to cross as if they were walking on concrete; who could heal people when they looked at a bronze snake; who could impregnate a virgin with the non-gender Holy Spirit; who could raise Lazarus from the dead; who could instantly heal all kinds of diseases; who could cast out demons with just two words, "Come out"; who could stop a fire from cremating three of His men, yet so hot that it killed the soldiers who got close enough to toss those three chaps into it; who could order a fish to shallow Jonah without hurting him, and then spit him out onto the beach is the SAME GOD WHO IS ALIVE AND WELL TODAY. He was not, is not, and never will become deaf or de-powered. Because that same God is your partner, make your prayers big.

The Sixth Phrase of the Lord's Prayer

"Our father who is in heaven, hallowed be your name, your kingdom come, your will be done on earth as it is in heaven. Give us today our daily bread. **Forgive our debts, as we forgive our debtors**" (Bold print mine). God loves to forgive sin He hates, because He loves us. Good fathers are like that, aren't they? And none is a better father than God.

The word "debt" refers to our sin against God and others. The word "debtors" refers to those who have sinned against God and us. The only comment Jesus made about the Lord's Prayer dealt with this phrase, "For if you forgive men when they sin against you, your heavenly Father will also forgive you. But if you do not forgive men their sins, your Father will not forgive your sins" (Matthew 6:14-15). One reason God forgives us is to let us taste the joy of being forgiven, so we will be His channels of forgiveness to others. That is one way to let our light so shine that people can see the nature of our Father in us (Matthew 5:16; Connect Ephesians 4:24 to 4:32-5:1-2). We owe it to God and to the person who has sinned against us to forgive.

The Prayer of Healing

One of the "daily needs" is for healing, but the objects of healing are varied which include the following:

1. Emotional healing, with grieving, loneliness, anger, and various complexes.
2. Spiritual healing, with rebellion, disobedience, sinfulness, apathy, and so on.

3. Physical healing. This includes small things such as fever, which Jesus was interested in healing. It also includes large and threatening situations, such as leprosy; genetic diseases or failures from birth, such as blindness; damaged bodies due to accidents and crime, such as the man on the road to Jericho, and so on.

Steps for praying for healing

1. Discern the healing needs of another.
2. Believe that God can heal and does heal. Perhaps one reason people in the church may quickly forget the names of people mentioned on Sunday is because they do not believe God really heals. How spiritually mature is that kind of thinking?

Why some are healed and some are not

A Christian will ALWAYS be healed either while living on earth or when transformed to heaven. We must leave with God the reasons some are healed here and others are not; but as we do, we need to remember that the mortality rate for all of us is 100%. It is one physical death for one physical birth until Christ returns.

Perhaps the only answer we have for those who lose a loved one to death even though there were intense and repeated prayers is that as high as the heavens are above us, so is God's love for us. We can trust God who loves us enough to say, "No" to Jesus who asked that He by pass the cross, and by doing so God said, "Yes" to us. Another reason some are not healed may be because God knows that some are powerful witnesses to others by the way they respond to and live with their physical problems, such as Job, Joni Erickson, the apostle Paul, and some you know.

Engaging in Prayers of Healing

1. Set aside a time to pray for specific healing for specific people, and for praying the sixth phrase of the Lord's Prayer.

2. Give God thanks for whatever answer is received.
3. Call for elders of the church to pray for the sick and to anoint them with oil. There is no supportable reason that the prayer ministry in James 5:13-14 does not continue today.
4. Keep asking without dropping it just because the healing has not come quickly.
5. Touch the person with whom you are praying, unless there are physical or sexual reasons not to do so. Touching is not to communicate there is power in the touch, but is a personal affirmation of your closeness, compassion, and concern for that person.
6. Enlist others to join in a concert of healing prayer for a specific person.
7. Never substitute medical and nutritional needs for prayer or prayer for medical and nutritional needs.
8. Record in a Prayer Journal the requests and answers.

Week 10

THE DISCIPLE OF THE PRAYER OF THANKSGIVING

PRAYER INFORMATION

A Reason Some May Use for Not Praying

"A million people may be talking with God the same time. How in the world would I get through, and how can God hear so many simultaneous prayers?"

It is impossible for the finite to understand the infinite beyond what He chooses to reveal. We do not need to understand how God can hear so many people praying at the same time. During the 19th century, who would have believed that hundreds of thousands of different conversations could travel through the same telephone wires to different locations without canceling out each other? Who would have believed that hundreds of thousands of different frequencies could travel through the air all around us with each frequency reaching its receiver? Realities thought impossible in the 19th and early 20th centuries are normal experiences in the 21st century. The list is nearly endless. The creativity and abilities of modern times do not reflect one millionth of one percent of God's creativity and abilities. That's one reason He is God ALMIGHTY. If you talk on the phone believing your voice will be heard by someone a thousand miles away when the lines or the air waves are crowded with countless other voices, then there is no reason to not chat with God during the same time others are.

The Concluding Phrases of the Lord's Prayer

"Our father who is in heaven, hallowed be your name, your kingdom come, your will be done on earth as it is in heaven. Give us today our daily bread. Forgive our debt, as we forgive our debtors.
And lead us not into temptations, but deliver us from the evil one, for yours is the kingdom and the power and the glory forever. Amen."

To ask God not to lead us into temptation is a way to say, "deliver us from the evil one." For those two statements are parallel, i.e. two statements communicating the same things with different words. Asking this from God includes the following:

1. Openly, honestly, and holistically share with the Father those environments and situations in which you are the most vulnerable. That may include places and people that are alluring to you or that may have you in their sights or grips.
2. Describe your feelings when you are with those people or in those locations.
3. Ask God to help you get out with a "Go."
4. Ask God to help you say, "No" to the pressure from specifically named people.
5. Ask God to escort you and stay with you until you are no longer affected.

6. Order the devil to buzz off.
7. Make a commitment to God not to return to those situations.
8. Thank God for being your internal companion, and affirm the fact that the One who is in you is stronger than the one who is in the world.

Engaging in Prayers of Thanksgiving

It is easy to let gratitude slip through the cracks when we live with so many benefits. It is easy to take for granted what we have. The following can help us develop an attitude of gratitude, which is the root for authentic thanksgiving:

1. Realize you are a receiver of EVERYTHING you have. Who among us can cultivate, plant, harvest, and process the food we eat? Who among us can cause the rain to fall and the sun to rise? Who among us can make our own clothes from scratch? Who among us can eradicate diseases? Who among us can build the roads on which we drive, and so on?
2. Spend time meditating on the various things you receive EVERY DAY, beginning with the start of the day. Brainstorm this in your own mind. For instance, did you wake up to a warm house in the winter? Did you refine the fuel, manufacture the furnace, design the thermostat, and so on?
3. As you meditate on 2 above, start expressing your gratitude to God for the many people that help make your life more comfortable, enjoyable, and secure.
4. Review your life from birth to the present, and share thanksgiving for being a recipient in every developmental stage.
5. Review what is presently a part of your life and express your gratitude for what you are receiving.
6. Reflect on ways God has benefited you, and express your gratitude.

Thanksgiving is not just verbal (words); it's also includes verbs (action).

Appendix II

Authentic thanks**giving** is always reflected in "thanks**living**." "Thanks**living**" includes the following at a minimum:

1. Humility with what you have received.
2. Generosity in sharing what you have received with and for others.
3. Responsibility for not abusing what you have received.
4. Investing what you have received into God's will and work on earth.
5. Living with and using what you have received the way He would.
6. Not wasting what you have received.

Those six are rooted in an **attitude of gratitude**.

Week 11

THE DISCIPLINE OF LOVE

Love and Spiritual Maturity

Love is an essential characteristic of Christlikeness. On the night Jesus was betrayed He said to His apostles, "A new commandment I give to you, that you love one another . . ." (John 13:34, NASB). This commandment was not new in its time, for it was recorded in Leviticus 19:18. But it was new in kind. That is, it was fresh in not being regularly used—hardly worn. Jesus did not leave the command with just "love one another," but added, "even as I have loved you, that you love one another." He wants His disciples to love as He loved and would love if He were here in person. And He is here through His Holy Spirit, "because God has poured his love into our hearts by the Holy Spirit" (Romans 5:5. NASB). To love exactly as Jesus loves is one way to measure how close we are to being conformed to the likeness of Christ.

The church at Corinth was filled with diverse relational problems because they had not matured. Paul nailed down their immaturity when he wrote that they were "mere infants in Christ" (1 Corinthians 3:1. NIV). They had no doubt been taught by some of the greatest teachers in that day—Apollos, Peter, Paul, and even Christ (1:12); they were enriched in speaking and knowledge (1:5); and they did not lack any spiritual gift (1:7). So what was missing? It was love. Thus, Paul's classic chapter on love was written to that congregation. It is easy to link the absence of one or more of the characteristics of love mentioned in 13:4-6 to one or more of the problems revealed in that letter. These early Christians evidently thought they had reached the height of maturity—already filled, being spiritually rich as spiritual kings, and superior to others (4:7-8). But Paul dropped the bomb on their arrogance when he wrote that without love they were nothing (13:1-3).

The Pervasiveness of love

The attributes of love and lovingkindness are mentioned throughout both the Old and New Testaments. Here are just a few ways love is connected to Christianity:

1. Love characterizes the first and second greatest commandments upon which all other commandments in the Old Testament are fulfilled (Matthew 22:35-40; Romans 13:8-10; Galatians 5:13-14).
2. Faith doesn't count unless it expresses itself through love (1 Corinthians 13:2; Galatians 5:6).
3. Love is **the** fruit of the Holy Spirit from which the other eight fruit attributes flow (Galatians 5:22-23).
4. Love is greater than faith and hope (1 Corinthians 13:13).
5. The goal of apostolic instruction is for love to flow from a pure heart, a good conscience, and a sincere faith (1 Timothy 1:5).
6. God has not given Christians "a spirit of timidity, but of power and love and discipline" (2 Timothy 1:7). Love links power to self-discipline.
7. Christ died on the cross because of God's love for the world (John 3:16; 1 John 4:10).
8. People can "see" God through His love, which is made complete when demonstrated through Christians (1 John 4:12).

9. Christians deceive themselves and others when they say they love God, but neglect their brothers and sisters in need (1 John 4:20-21; 2:10-11. Note: The Greek word for hate means to love someone less than another, or to simply neglect or ignore a person.)
10. No one can fathom the depth of what God is able to do when Christians are rooted and grounded in love (Ephesians 3:14-21).
11. Love is the Christian's motivation for serving one another and others (Galatians 5:13).
12. Christians are to prove their love to God by their generous stewardship with finances (2 Corinthians 8:24. Study this verse in the context of the preceding 23 verses).
13. Christians are to love all other Christians (Colossians 1:4; 1 John 4:21-5:2).
14. Christians are to love not only in word, what we say, but also in deeds, what we do (1 John 3:18).
15. Christians are to speak the truth in love (Ephesians 4:15). We are to love those with whom we speak the gospel. We are not to speak in an attitude and tone of voice that communicates we are glad certain people may go to hell.
16. The royal commandment is that we love one another (James 2:8).
17. Love does not hurt others (Romans 13:8-10).
18. Love disciplines others (Hebrews 12:4-12).

Love is a Many Splendrous Thing

In English we use one little four-letter word to express different levels of love. For instance, we may say, "I love my car" and, "I love my wife or husband." But we surely have a different level of love in mind for those two different recipients. When our car gets old and starts wearing out, we trade it for a newer and better model. However, some seem to have that same level of love for their mate as for their car—get a newer and better model.

The Greek language used the following four different words to express four different levels of love:

1. **Eros.** Contrary to what is popularly taught, *eros* is not restricted to being sexual or sensual. Rather, *eros* is always one-way love—back to self. *Eros* may do something good for someone else, but only for what the giver plans to get out of it for self. A person is expressing *eros* if that person gives millions of dollars to an institution primarily to get his or her name on a building, plus getting a tax credit. There is nothing wrong with the benefactor getting a tax break, or with the name on a building. Doing so is not *eros* unless those self-benefits were the reasons for such love-gifts. A one-way U-turn line drawn from self back to self depicts this self-only centered kind of love.
2. **Agape.** This is also a one-way love, but to and for the other person's benefit. This kind of love will engage in the following: (A) Sees a need and moves to meet it. The person who is not able to personally meet it will find other ways, such as others who are able to meet the need, as those who carried their paralytic friend to Jesus did. (B) Does not count the cost. (C) Does not calculate whether or not the person is worth having the need met. The issue is not the worth of the person, but the need of that person. (D) Does not calculate what the giver will get out of it for self. (E) Makes decisions for the other person's benefit. This is an unselfish need-meeting love. Sexual intimacy between married mates should be an expression of *agape*, as the Greek translation of Genesis 24:66 revealed. Sexual intimacy expresses *agape* when both demonstrate the characteristics of 1 Corinthians 13:4-6 in their sharing. A one-way line drawn from self to and for another depicts this love. Contrary to popular teaching this love is not necessarily unconditional. Pagans can express *agape*. Jesus corrected both of those erroneous teachings in Matthew 5:48 and Luke 6:32. Whether or not *agape* is unconditional depends upon the person loving, not upon the word itself. God is the perfect model of expressing *agape* unconditionally, for He is not a respecter of persons.
3. **Philos.** This is always a two-way love. It is the mutual affection, respect, and connection between friends. It is the friendship love. It is the "I like you" love. That is why it is a two-way love. It takes

two to establish and keep the friendship alive. Two different lines drawn from each person to the other person like a two-lane highway depict this love. We are commanded to like each other. Every time the Bible commands brotherly love, it is commanding that we initiate affection for our brothers (Romans 12:10; Hebrews 13:1). While we may initiate *philos* love, there is no guarantee it will be received well and returned. Remember, it is a two-way kind of love. However, all of us need to be open to be liked by others. Perhaps we need to be more kind and less rude, more accepting and less rejecting, and more gracious and less judgmental, and so on. "Brotherly love" is the Greek word *philadelphia,* which is the word *philos* connected to the Greek word for "brother." God expresses *philos* love as well as *agape*. He not only loves us with the kind that sees our needs and meets them, but also He also likes us. See God expressing *philos* love in John 5:20 and 16:27. We are commanded not only to have *philos* for our brother, but also for God (1 Corinthians 16:22). Jesus also expressed *philos* (John 11:36; 20:2; Revelation 3:19). It is anti-biblical to say, "I have to love you, but I don't have to like you."
4. **Storge.** This is the love among members of the same family, which is a bond unlike any other. This love is depicted with a circle that connects all members of the same family and with arrows on the perimeter of the circle pointing to each other.

The Four Loves in One Person

From time to time and from situation to situation, all of us express these four different kinds of love. It is important that we become aware of which kind we are expressing to others, and which kind we are receiving from others. Our relationships can be weakened or strengthened by the kind of love we are giving and receiving. It is possible to share *philos* with a friend but not *agape,* just as is possible to express *agape* to someone for whom we have no *philos*. It is possible to marry someone with only *eros*, but that kind of love cannot maintain a positive relationship. It is even possible to express *storge* with a family member, but not *philos* or *agape*. We need to love in many different contexts.

Engaging the Discipline of Love

1. Practice identifying which of the above four loves you demonstrate.
2. Practice identifying which kind of love you received from another.
3. Note your emotions when giving and receiving a specific kind of love.
4. Notice different kinds of love given and received by others.
5. Commit to eliminate the *eros* kind of love.
6. Commit to expand your circle of *philos* friendships.
7. Stay alert for people with special needs to which you can apply one of the three positive kinds of loves.
8. Each day journal the kinds of love you demonstrated and received.
9. Analyze why one kind is more dominant than another.

Appendix III

Asssessing Personal Spiritual Formation Into Christlikeness

Value of a Personal Assessment

1. An assessment tool is essential to determine the effectiveness of a spiritual development program.
2. An assessment tool measures a person's progress in spiritual formation.
3. An assessment tool measures a person's strengths and weaknesses.
4. An assessment tool helps a person identify and develop the attitudes and activities needed to advance toward Christlikeness.

Instructions for this Assessment Tool

1. Instead of marking this form, keep it clean, copy it, and re-test yourself for years to come. If you are not able to copy it, put each category on another sheet of paper. Under each category place as many numbers as are the items in that category to be scored.

Example: under "Meditation" list 1, 2, 3, 4, 5. Then place your score next to the corresponding number.
2. Let your first inclination determine your score for each item.
3. After completing the entire assessment, do the following:

- Add the points scored under each category to get the total for each category
- Divide the total by the number of items scored. For instance, if you scored two 4's, two 3's, and one 2 under "Meditation", the total is 16. Divided by 5 for the average of 3.2.

Scoring Your Spiritual Maturity

The following scores reflect stages of maturity:

1 = an infant, needing to feed on the milk of the Word with lots of help from others.
2 = a toddler, doing some walking, but needing lots of input.
3 = an adolescent, living as a disciple able to disciple others in some area of spiritual formation.
4 = an adult, conformed to the likeness of Christ in that category, which is worth others imitating.

Follow-up

After calculating the stage of maturity in each category, do the following:

1. Prioritize the weak stages according to the ones that need most attention.
2. Devise a method to advance maturity in that category.
3. Set a timetable for doing what needs to be done in that category.
4. Decide a schedule for re-testing—every year, every two years, and so on.
5. Enjoy growing up to Christlikeness. As you grow, you will put a smile on God's face.

Appendix III

PERSONAL ASSESSMENT

The following are formatted on a 1-4 grid.

1-not at all important (or I do not at all agree), **2**- slightly important (or I slightly agree), **3**- quite important (or I mostly agree), **4**- greatly important (or I totally agree).

Circle the number that describes your current thoughts and activities.

Meditation

1. It is important to set aside time each day for meditation.   1 2 3 4
2. Meditation should be done less than 15 minutes a day.   1 2 3 4
3. Meditation should be done at least 15-30 minutes a day.   1 2 3 4
4. I mediate daily.   1 2 3 4
5. I feel the presence of God when I meditate.   1 2 3 4

Total Score_____; Divided by 5 =_____

Connections

With a specific congregation

1. I attend a church service at least once a week.   1 2 3 4
2. I attend a church service more than once a week.   1 2 3 4
3. I attend a Bible study group.   1 2 3 4
4. I attend a small group.   1 2 3 4
5. I am involved in a specific service function in the church.   1 2 3 4
6. I am a leader in a specific ministry of the church.   1 2 3 4
7. I give some of my income to the church.
    a. Less then 5%   1
    b. At least 5%   2
    c. At least 10%   3
    d. More than 10%   4
8. For me, the church is as essential as the Bible.   1 2 3 4

Total Score_____Divided by 8=_____.

Becoming Fully Human In An Inhuman World

With Self

1. I believe in myself.   1 2 3 4
2. I am satisfied with the way I look.   1 2 3 4
3. I believe I am worthy of God's love.   1 2 3 4
4. I believe I am worthy of being loved by others.   1 2 3 4
5. I love myself.   1 2 3 4
6. I know the gifts/charisma I have.   1 2 3 4
7. I like the gifts I have.   1 2 3 4

Total Score_____Divided by 7=_____.

With the Heavenly Father

1. I regularly seek the presence of the Father.   1 2 3 4
2. I like the Father.   1 2 3 4
3. I believe the Father listens to me.   1 2 3 4
4. I believe the Father is for me.   1 2 3 4
5. I believe the Father is close to me when I pray.   1 2 3 4
6. I live to please the Father in all I do and decisions I make. 1 2 3 4
7. I want the Father to watch me in my private life.   1 2 3 4
8. I seek the Father's influence when I make decisions.   1 2 3 4
9. I want the Father's influence when I am in trouble.   1 2 3 4
10. I feel the influence of God when I work at my job.   1 2 3 4
11. There are times I feel God communicating with me.   1 2 3 4

Total Score_____Divided by 11=_____.

With Jesus

1. I feel the presence of Jesus in my life.   1 2 3 4
2. I intentionally try to be like Jesus.   1 2 3 4
3. I believe I can talk to Jesus.   1 2 3 4
4. I talk with Jesus.   1 2 3 4
5. I believe Jesus lives inside me.   1 2 3 4
6. I believe Jesus likes me.   1 2 3 4
7. I intentionally make decisions to please Jesus.   1 2 3 4
8. I believe Jesus lives for me and goes to bat for me with the Father. 1 2 3 4
9. I know I am becoming more like Jesus in all my relationships.   1 2 3 5

Total Score_____Divided by 9=_____.

Appendix III

With the Holy Spirit

1. I experience the presence of the Holy Spirit.   1 2 3 4
2. I believe the Holy Spirit exists to help guide me.   1 2 3 4
3. I have experienced the influence of the Holy Spirit.
   - When making decisions.   1 2 3 4
   - When meditating.   1 2 3 4
   - When being tempted.   1 2 3 4
   - When in trouble.   1 2 3 4
   - When reading the Bible.   1 2 3 4
   - When having problems.   1 2 3 4
   - When having a good time with others.   1 2 3 4
   - When having a good time when alone.   1 2 3 4

Total Score_____Divided by 10=_____.

With Friends

1. It is important to have both Christian and non-Christian friends. 1 2 3 4
2. I keep in close contact with friends.   1 2 3 4
3. I am transparent with at least one very close friend.   1 2 3 4
4. I do not camouflage my Christianity when I am with friends.   1 2 3 4
5. I never share gossip even with my closest friends.   1 2 3 4
6. I have at least one friend to whom I am accountable.   1 2 3 4
7. I invite my friends to church.   1 2 3 4
8. I have friends who belong to different denominations.   1 2 3 4
9. My friends trust me.   1 2 3 4
10. My friends know I am a disciple of Christ,
    and they know my values.   1 2 3 4
11. I do not play the "holier than you" game
    with non-Christian friends.   1 2 3 4

Total Score_____Divided by 11=_____.

The Bible

1. I believe the Bible is God's inspired word.   1 2 3 4
2. I believe the original manuscripts were without any errors.   1 2 3 4
3. I believe the morals in the Bible are absolutes for me.   1 2 3 4
4. I believe the morals in the Bible are absolutes for all people.   1 2 3 4

5. I believe I can learn God's Word from many different versions.   1 2 3 4
6. I follow a plan to read the Bible
    a. Hardly ever.   1
    b. Occasionally.   2
    c. Regularly.   3
    d. Reading through the entire Bible at least once a year.   4

7. I take notes when I read the Bible.   1 2 3 4
8. I sometimes spend 15 minutes or more meditating on just one verse.   1 2 3 4
9. I often pray over verses as I read.   1 2 3 4
10. I make changes in my attitudes and actions because of the Bible's influence.   1 2 3 4
11. God speaks to me through the Bible.   1 2 3 4

Total Score_____Divided by 11=_____.

Prayer

1. I believe prayer can change things.   1 2 3 4
2. I believe God is open to act on my prayers.   1 2 3 4
3. I am very transparent to God when I pray.   1 2 3 4
4. Because God is my partner, I make some prayers very big.   1 2 3 4
5. I pray when nothing is going well.   1 2 3 4
6. I have experienced specific answers to prayers of mine or of others.   1 2 3 4
7. I pray when I am facing temptations.   1 2 3 4
8. I pray when having troubles.   1 2 3 4
9. I believe God listens carefully to my prayers.   1 2 3 4
10. I believe God performs miracles in answer to prayers.   1 2 3 4
11. The accumulated time I pray each day is
    a. 1-3 minutes, if that long   1
    b. Less than 15 minutes.   2
    c. At least 30 minutes to an hour   3
    d. An hour or more   4
13. I pray to God about anything, such as the following:
    a. Temptations   1 2 3 4
    b. Confession of sins.   1 2 3 4
    c. My work.   1 2 3 4
    d. Complaining to God.   1 2 3 4

e.	Questioning God.	1 2 3 4
f.	Love talk to God.	1 2 3 4
g.	Praise talk.	1 2 3 4

Total Score_____Divided by 18=_____

Conscience

1. I know in what areas I am weak when tempted. — 1 2 3 4
2. I usually resist temptations. — 1 2 3 4
3. I work to strengthen my vulnerable areas. — 1 2 3 4
4. I am not a consistent complainer. — 1 2 3 4
5. I do not gossip. — 1 2 3 4
6. I do not engage in homosexual activities. — 1 2 3 4
7. I do not engage in heterosexual activities outside marriage. — 1 2 3 4
8. I do not look at or listen to pornography. — 1 2 3 4
9. I do not cheat. — 1 2 3 4
10. I do not lie. — 1 2 3 4
11. I believe in helping others when I can. — 1 2 3 4
12. I don't hold grudges. — 1 2 3 4
13. I am a forgiving person. — 1 2 3 4
14. I believe my life is in control. — 1 2 3 4
15. I believe my tongue is in control. — 1 2 3 4
16. I believe my sex life is in control. — 1 2 3 4

Total Score_____Divided by 16=_____

Beliefs

1. God knows all about me. — 1 2 3 4
2. God knows every minute detail about my future. — 1 2 3 4
3. God knows my thoughts. — 1 2 3 4
4. God loves me. — 1 2 3 4
5. God likes me. — 1 2 3 4
6. Faith is to be linked to doing something. — 1 2 3 4
7. Repentance is necessary for forgiveness. — 1 2 3 4
8. I am forgiven by God. — 1 2 3 4
9. I am to forgive others—regardless. — 1 2 3 4
10. God can still do miracles. — 1 2 3 4
11. God still does miracles. — 1 2 3 4

12. The Holy Spirit is alive on earth.   1 2 3 4
13. God, Jesus, or the Holy Spirit can pop thoughts into my mind. 1 2 3 4
14. Christians can conform to the likeness of Christ while on earth. 1 2 3 4
15. My non-church activities can be ministries.   1 2 3 4
16. It is essential to be a functioning member of a congregation.   1 2 3 4
17. One ministry in the church is as important as any
    other ministry in the church.   1 2 3 4
18. Jesus is the only Savior of anyone in the world.   1 2 3 4
19. Only Christians can be saved.   1 2 3 4
20. Confession is essential for being forgiven.   1 2 3 4
21. We are to confess our sins to God.   1 2 3 4
22. God speaks to me through others.   1 2 3 4
23. God speaks through me to others.   1 2 3 4
24. Heaven is an eternal reality.   1 2 3 4
25. Hell is an eternal reality.   1 2 3 4
26. The devil is as real as God.   1 2 3 4
27. Jesus lived, died, rose, and will return.   1 2 3 4
28. Jesus intercedes for me to the Father.   1 2 3 4
29. I need to be involved in a church to mature as a Christian.   1 2 3 4
30. My service in the church reflects my love to God and others.   1 2 3 4

Total Score_____Divided by 30=_____

Service

1. I serve in at least one ministry in the church.   1 2 3 4
2. I serve in at least one activity in a non-church community.   1 2 3 4
3. I support evangelism with money, prayers, and practices.   1 2 3 4
4. I support mission work in other places around the world
   with money, prayers, activities, and so on.   1 2 3 4
5. My secular job is service to people and thus is service to God.   1 2 3 4
6. I do not allow my services to be in competition against
   services of others.   1 2 3 4

Total Score_____Divided by 6=_____.

Appendix III

Preferences

1. I am open to and would encourage the following to serve in the church in accordance with their charismas (gifts from God):
   a. Single adults. 1 2 3 4
   b. Divorcees. 1 2 3 4
   c. Divorced and remarried. 1 2 3 4
   d. One who has had an abortion. 1 2 3 4
   e. An ethnic person who is not well represented by the same ethnic group either in the church or the immediate surrounding community. 1 2 3 4
   f. A former homosexual. 1 2 3 4
   g. An unwed mother. 1 2 3 4
   h. Single parents. 1 2 3 4
   i. A homeless Christian. 1 2 3 4
   j. A person with several tattoos. 1 2 3 4
   k. A person with several body piercings. 1 2 3 4
   l. An Asian person. 1 2 3 4
   m. An Hispanic person. 1 2 3 4
   n. A Black person. 1 2 3 4
   o. Teenagers. 1 2 3 4
   p. A recovered alcoholic.

2. It is good for the church to mix its membership among several different ethnic groups living in the geographical area. 1 2 3 4
3. The church should inclusive to all with a variety of music styles. 1 2 3 4
4. All Christians are ministers and all ministries are valuable. 1 2 3 4

Total Score_____Divided by 19=_____

The Completed Assessment Score_____Divided by 161=_____

See The Unscientific Interpretation of the Score on page 162

Developed by Knofel Staton, D. D; D..Min. , Hope International University. Fullerton, California